FINDING GOD IN A WORLD COME OF AGE

Past Light on Present Life: Theology, Ethics, and Spirituality

Roger Haight, SJ, Alfred Pach III,
and *Amanda Avila Kaminski,* series editors

These volumes are offered to the academic community of teachers and learners in the fields of Christian history, theology, ethics, and spirituality. They introduce classic texts by authors whose contributions have markedly affected the development of Christianity, especially in the West. The texts are accompanied by an introductory essay on context and key themes and followed by an interpretation that dialogically engages the original message with the issues of ethics, theology, and spirituality in the present.

Finding God in a World Come of Age

KARL RAHNER AND JOHANN BAPTIST METZ

EDITED AND WITH COMMENTARY BY
*Roger Haight, SJ, Alfred Pach III,
and Amanda Avila Kaminski*

FORDHAM UNIVERSITY PRESS   NEW YORK 2024

This series has been generously supported by a theological education grant from the E. Rhodes and Leona B. Carpenter Foundation.

"Reflections on the Unity of the Love of Neighbor and the Love of God" is reprinted from Karl Rahner, *Theological Investigations 6: Concerning Vatican Council II* (Baltimore: Helicon Press, 1974), 231–249. © Karl Rahner. Reprinted by arrangement with The Crossroad Publishing Company. www.crossroadpublishing.com

"Considerations on the Active Role of the Person in the Sacramental Event" is reprinted from Karl Rahner, *Theological Investigations 14: Ecclesiology, Questions in the Church, the Church in the World* (New York: Seabury Press, 1976), 161–184. © Karl Rahner. Reprinted by arrangement with The Crossroad Publishing Company. www.crossroadpublishing.com

"Transcendental-Idealist or Narrative-Practical Christianity? Theology and Christianity's Contemporary Identity Crisis" is reprinted from Johann Baptist Metz, *Faith in History and Society: Toward a Practical Fundamental Theology* (New York: Crossroad, 2007), 144–155. © Johann Baptist Metz. Reprinted by arrangement with The Crossroad Publishing Company. www.crossroadpublishing.com

Fordham University Press has no responsibility for the persistence or accuracy of URLs for external or third-party Internet websites referred to in this publication and does not guarantee that any content on such websites is, or will remain, accurate or appropriate.

Fordham University Press also publishes its books in a variety of electronic formats. Some content that appears in print may not be available in electronic books.

Visit us online at www.fordhampress.com.

Library of Congress Cataloging-in-Publication Data available online at https://catalog.loc.gov.

Printed in the United States of America

26 25 24   5 4 3 2 1

First edition

Contents

FINDING GOD IN A WORLD COME OF AGE

I

Introduction to the Lives
and Works of Karl Rahner
and Johann Baptist Metz

During his days in prison in Berlin, Dietrich Bonhoeffer had time to read and reflect on the Enlightenment and to ask the question of how Christians might live "in a world come of age."[1] The phrase symbolizes the challenge of modernity for theology. One can interpret Karl Rahner's and Johann Baptist Metz's theological writings as addressing that question. We begin with the authorship of Karl Rahner: His work is massive and comprehensive; he poked his intellectual finger into everything. One can only humbly offer a brief introduction to the theologian and his thought and be careful not to oversimplify the unique character of his language, a complex hybrid distilled from various sources. But Rahner's thought carries insight deeply into the subject matter of the relationship between God and human existence shaped by Christian faith in a modern age.

The logical moves of this Introduction are straightforward. It begins by spreading out the chronology of Rahner's formation and education. The next step singles out a few basic concepts and principles of Rahner's that enable one to appreciate the patterns of thought that animate the texts chosen to represent his spirituality. The third part offers a map of the argument of the texts. His insight, which sometimes seems to be hidden in technical terms, often corresponds to common sense from a present-day perspective. The hope is that the overview will enable the deeper appreciation of how Rahner opens up the spiritual value of the interaction between the spheres of ethics and worship.

Rahner's Early Life and Education. Karl Rahner was born on March 5, 1904, in Freiburg in southwestern Germany, and his early education was in the city. In 1922, at the age of eighteen, he followed his brother Hugo, three years older, in joining the Jesuits.[2] For two years in the novitiate in Feldkirch, Austria, he was introduced to Ignatian spirituality, which had a distinct influence on his theology. After another year of study, he moved to the Jesuit school of philosophy in Pullach, outside Munich, where he studied scholastic philosophy from 1925 to 1927. But he also read Kant and the Belgian Jesuit philosopher Joseph Maréchal who, in the spirit of Maurice Blondel, had negotiated an integration between the Kantian turn to subjectivity and the thought of Thomas Aquinas. This was followed by two years back in Feldkirch, where he taught Latin for two years.

Rahner began his formal training in theology in 1929 in the Jesuit seminary in Holland. Ordained in 1932, he studied one more year of formal theology and did a final year of Jesuit formation in the south of Austria. Then, finally, in 1934 he was sent by the Jesuits back to the university in his home, Freiburg, to do a degree in philosophy.[3]

These two years at Freiburg were especially formative for the development of Rahner's theology. During them he participated in the seminar of Martin Heidegger. He then wrote an existentialist interpretation of the metaphysics of knowing in dialogue with a seminal text of Thomas Aquinas, and thus he developed a "transcendental" understanding of the character of the human person as constituted in the physical world but fundamentally open to transcendent reality.[4] In mid-1936

Rahner transferred to Innsbruck, where he finished a doctoral thesis in historical theology in the early church. He received his doctorate in theology in December of 1936 and began teaching at the University of Innsbruck in the fall of 1937. But during the summer of that year he gave a series of fifteen lectures in Salzburg that became another seminal statement of his basic vision, a philosophy of religion, entitled *Hearer of the Word.*[5]

Rahner's post on the theology faculty of the University of Innsbruck did not last long: In 1938, Nazi Germany invaded Austria, and the university closed the theology department. Rahner taught for another year in the Jesuit building there, but that was closed a year later. In the fall of 1939 he transferred to a pastoral institute in Vienna, where he taught, wrote, and lectured until 1944.

> In summer 1944, his public activity in Vienna was over. As the Russians advanced nearer to the city, the terror of the *Schutzstaffel* (SS) increased. Rahner had to leave Vienna. In July 1944, he came to a small village in Lower Bavaria and there took over the pastoral care of the local people and many refugees. After the entry of the Americans, he was called in August 1945 to the Jesuit college of St. John Berchman in Pullach, where the study of theology had just been resumed. There he taught dogmatic theology and also did a great deal of work in the badly bombed city of Munich.[6]

In 1948, Rahner was called back to the University of Innsbruck, where he taught until 1964. During these years he was also engaged as an "expert" theologian in service of the Second Vatican Council (1962–65).

During the years after World War II, through Vatican II and afterward, Rahner's theological creativity took off.[7] Besides teaching, Rahner had a vigorous schedule of invited lectures, writing essays, and cooperating in editing and writing theological encyclopedias. His scope was vast: In the 1950s he entered the discussion of the relation between theology and science; he also considered the relation of Christianity to other religions. Both of these topics have become subjects of major discussion today. But he chiefly engaged doctrinal and spiritual themes in a new, creative way.

Before we turn to some of the fundamental theological conceptions that were gained early in Rahner's formation, a schematic outline of his movements will round off his career. In 1964 he occupied the chair of theology held by Romano Guardini at the University of Munich. Beginning in 1967, he taught at the University of Münster until his retirement in 1971. Rahner remained active as a professor emeritus at Munich until 1981, when he moved to Innsbruck. He died there in 1984 a few weeks after his eightieth birthday.

Some Basic Concepts in Rahner's Thought. It goes without saying that the choice of a few basic ideas of Rahner's do not add up to an adequate introduction to his thinking. But certain distinctive principles can help draw the curtains on a horizon that, once it is in place, helps to provide the deeper dimensions of perspective that make Rahner's thought resonate with personal experience. This procedure risks offending by omission; so much lies unsaid here. Also, the translation of Rahner's formulations into less technical and more accessible language risks oversimplification. The hope is that a quest for clarity in short direct propositions does not positively distort the direction and scope of his vision.

(i) "Transcendental" refers to the universal structure of the operations of the human subject. The term *transcendental* has a few meanings in Rahner, but two are most significant. First, it is a Kantian term that refers to a universal *a priori*, or always simply given, structure of human consciousness. In this sense, it often simply means universal—that is, applying not just to my consciousness but going beyond any particular human consciousness and referring to all human consciousness, to the structure of humanity itself in the processes of knowing, willing, and acting. The transcendental structure of the human spirit is a constant referent in Rahner's thinking. It is his "turn to the subject"; it defines his theology as "anthropocentric" in its method.

A second meaning of "transcendental" refers to a "going beyond"—beyond the finite sphere of objects, toward that which exceeds all creation and implies infinity. This transcendence is also transcendental in the first sense: All human consciousness possesses a dimension that reaches out toward and actually comes in contact with the infinite, at least implicitly if not psychologically. *Transcendental* and *transcendence* are common Rahnerian terms, and either of these meanings or both together can usually be discerned from the context.

(ii) The world in its human history enjoys God's grace or self-communication from the beginning. Rahner's building the case for this and employing it in many of his theological arguments may be his most important contribution to Catholic theology. Today it is taken for granted. His argument is simple but profound. God wills that all people be saved. Two things flow from this: first, that this must mark human existence in some way; human beings are not the same as we would be if God did not will universal salvation. The other is that, if God wills the salvation of all, God must supply the means by which that could happen. But that "means" is commonly understood to be saving grace. Therefore, God must offer God's saving grace to all people, for their acceptance or rejection. The conclusion is that the whole human race enjoys the offer of God's grace or self-communication from the beginning of the human species. And human beings must have within themselves the ability to find and respond to this grace.

Rahner is often called a theologian of grace. His distinctive view of the world is the opposite of what was derived from Augustine: The whole of history operates within the embrace of God's saving presence rather than sin. As a fundamental outlook, this position transforms everything in an Augustinian world.

(iii) All human knowing and willing implies unthematic or not explicitly conscious openness to God. This basic premise is established by Rahner by his transcendental analysis of the human subject, first in his original thesis that was rejected, *Spirit in the World*, and also in *Hearer of the Word*. By a careful phenomenological description and analysis of knowing and willing, Rahner shows how these basic dynamisms of human existence are insatiable; they reach out to all things as true, as good, as "being" to be appropriated. An analysis of this dynamism shows that it contains a dimension of infinity. This appears by contrast with the limits and boundaries of the finitude of all it directly encounters. This awareness of a "beyond the finite" implicitly (Rahner would say "unthematically") introduces a real contact with the infinite. The very possibility of grasping that all reality together is still finite reveals an implicit knowledge of, or participation in, a horizon of infinity. Infinity is the implicit absence of all limits that makes finitude appear as such.[8] Such is the transparency of the human spirit to itself and its openness and participation in absolute or infinite reality.

(iv) Salvation by grace through love has always been a possibility for all human beings from the beginning. Just as Luther said that salvation is received by grace through faith, Rahner's view is that, more generally, salvation is by grace through love. This love includes faith and hope within itself, as Luther's faith includes hope and love of God. But, for Rahner, love better describes the human response that is possible for all human beings, even those who are atheists, who nevertheless implicitly open themselves in receptiveness to God's saving presence. For Rahner, this implicit self-transcending love represents a kind of anonymous faith. A loving response to other persons is the way human beings respond most generally to the universal loving presence of God to all. This theological position will be explained in the readings; it is very basic and figures in the arguments of both of Rahner's texts.

These distinctions do not fully open the door to Rahner's theological house, but they will help clarify some of the lines of his thinking.

The Texts of Rahner. Two texts have been chosen to represent a central element of Karl Rahner's analysis of Christian spirituality. The first provides a theological analysis of how, in responding to a fellow human being out of love, one is actually also responding to God. In the second, Rahner gives a rationale for formal worship. In a word, he shows how we bring the union with God manifested in everyday life to formal worship and express gratitude for it. The first essay lays the foundation for the second, which alters a "gas station" view of weekly worship.

What follows are two maps of the line of argument of Rahner's two essays in a series of propositions. They are plainly spoken and should be read in the light provided by the key ideas just visited.

(i) In the first essay, Rahner announces up front what he seeks to show in the essay: Genuine love of neighbor is love of God, whether one realizes it or not.[9] If such a love of another person is genuinely altruistic, the two are equivalent. The rest of the essay explains this proposition of the gospel.

(ii) Authentic human actions unfold within a horizon of infinite scope. Something is "explicitly" conscious when a person clearly envisions it; something "implicit" may be at work when one does not attend to it. The implicit factor may be what is most important. For example, the little boy in a toyshop may express an explicit desire for this one toy, but he really wants all of them. This deeper level of the direction of our actions Rahner calls a "transcendental horizon," which indicates a level of intentionality that may not be explicitly experienced but is present and operative in all acts of knowing and willing. This horizon is the ultimate goal or direction of all human actions that are actually searching for the ultimate truth and goodness. Thus Rahner can say, "[W]here the whole 'transcendental' depth of inter-human love is realized and represented . . . , there such a love is also necessarily a conscious [but not self-consciously so] love of God and has God as its reflex motive. . . ."[10]

(iii) God's personal presence as grace (Holy Spirit) is operative in all human self-transcendence. This is another of Rahner's foundational building blocks explained earlier: "[W]herever man posits a positively moral action in the full exercise of his free self-disposal, this act is a positive supernatural salvific [or grace-filled] act in the actual economy of salvation even when its *a posteriori* object and the explicitly given *a posteriori* motive do not spring tangibly from the positive revelation of God's Word but are in this sense 'natural.' This is so because God in virtue of his universal salvific will offers everyone his supernaturally divinizing grace and thus elevates the positively moral act of man."[11] Rahner effectively offers a theology of justification through love, not *by* love, but by the grace that enables authentic love. Authentic love essentially comprises the assistance of God's saving grace.

(iv) Love of neighbor is the primary and fundamental moral action of a human being. Rahner's point here is that neighbor love is not just another moral act but defines the character of morality. He supports the claim with three points expressed in dense technical language. First, humans are social animals; they interrelate by nature. Second, of all human interrelationships, the "act of personal love for another human being is therefore the all-embracing basic act of man which gives meaning, direction and measure to everything else."[12] This is so because, when it is authentic, such an act defines a fundamental orientation away from selfish introversion and toward a respect that reaches outward for what transcends the self. Third, it follows that "the one basic human act, where it takes place positively, is the love of neighbor understood as *caritas*, i.e., as a love of neighbor whose movement is directed towards the God of eternal life."[13]

(v) Response to the neighbor is a self-disposition that constitutes one's ultimate moral posture. This proposition does not advance the argument but appeals to Augustine's theology of grace to justify how an authentic act of love for another entails grace or divine help. In a way, he is reiterating one of his initial premises—namely, that if "in the present economy of salvation and on account of the universal salvific will of God *every* radically free moral act becomes a saving act through grace and is thus orientated towards the immediate presence to God, then this must be true *a fortiori* of the basic moral act which integrates everything, viz. the love of our neighbor."[14]

(vi) The only possible contact with God is through a this-worldly medium. This straightforward statement lies hidden in Rahner's technical prose. He is responding to the objection that the highest human act is not love of neighbor but love of God. But he replies that God is not like another object of this world, so that one could compare loving God with loving theater or even a spouse. Because God is transcendent, God cannot be approached directly or immediately but only indirectly or through the mediation of the world. God enters our consciousness as the *ground* of our experience of this world; or, shifting the metaphor, in an experience of infinity as the negation of all boundaries and limits, or as the infinite horizon of all our finite experiences of knowing and willing. And the highest medium for the love directed to God is love of neighbor; it is in love of neighbor that the transcendental contact with God actually happens or materializes itself.

(vii) Love of neighbor is the primary way of responding to God's presence in grace. The conditions for this strong thesis of Rahner's are now in place. The "explicit love of neighbor is the primary act of the love of God. The love of God [in this love of neighbor] unreflectively [unthematically] but really and always intends God in supernatural [grace-filled] transcendentality in the love of neighbor as such, and even the explicit love of God is still borne by that opening in trusting love to the whole of reality which takes place in the love of neighbor. It is radically true, i.e. by an ontological and not merely 'moral' or psychological necessity, that whoever does not love the brother whom he 'sees' also cannot love God whom he does not see, and that one can love God whom one does not see only *by* loving one's visible brother lovingly."[15] Thus Rahner translates into philosophical theological terms themes that come directly from the Johannine writings in the New Testament.

(viii) Therefore, love of neighbor is love of God. This statement of the original thesis is the conclusion of his argument. It responds to Bonhoeffer's question: How are we to envisage Christian spirituality in a world come of age? But it needs more discussion, and the following essay partially supplies it.

The second of Rahner's two essays focuses on formal worship.[16] Although he is talking about sacraments generally, his attention falls on the eucharist. What he says about the eucharist can be transferred to liturgy generally, or the worship service, or the sermon. The theology of the preached word and that of sacraments are structurally analogous: They both sensibly mediate consciousness and the effectiveness of God's grace. The issue then is this: How does assembly for public worship relate to everyday Christian spiritual life? Once again, the map charts Rahner's development with propositional statements of the steps of his argument.

(i) Should sacrament and formal liturgy be considered isolated encounters with God? Rahner begins with a negative portrait of the view that is in place as a contrast to his own. In a standard account, sacramental encounter with God stands over against life in the world where things appear monotonous and God remote. Formal worship is intended to fuel one for the week's secular activities. One seeks a God-fix. But it doesn't work. The gap is too great. Even frequent reception of the sacraments does not resolve the problem but rather exacerbates it by widening the separation of the spheres of Sunday worship and life during the week. Secular life, which occupies most of our time, ends up rendering liturgical worship escapist or episodic or empty.

(ii) Rahner provides a basis for a new model: Recognizing God's universal gracious and saving presence in the world offers new understanding of the role of formal worship. Rahner makes a strategic move here: Instead of reading the dynamics of spiritual life as moving from liturgy to life in the world, he reverses the direction. One moves from union with God in the world to liturgy where one's life in the world is celebrated. The basis for this reinterpretation picks up principles from the first essay—namely, that God is present to and encountered primarily in the everyday life of social relationships. Christian life unfolds in a secular world. Liturgy brings this life in the world to formal representation and reflection before God.

To support this constructive step, Rahner lays out his theory of God's universal saving self-presence and grace to all of history. A positive human response to God's presence occurs in every act of self-transcendence as in love of neighbor. God's saving grace "and divine life is present *everywhere* where the individual does not close himself to God."[17] "The world is constantly and ceaselessly possessed by grace from its innermost roots, from the innermost personal center of the spiritual subject."[18] Formal religious activities cannot be thought of as intermittent moments in which God intervenes in the world from outside it. Liturgy has to be thought of in relation to the deep moments in secular life where we confront the deepest mystery of life and, in it, encounter God.

(iii) Sacrament and formal liturgy are symbolic representations of the liturgy of the world. The sacraments and the liturgical celebrations of the church "constitute the manifestation of the holiness and the redeemed state of the secular dimension of human life and of the world."[19] They are signposts or road-markers indicating that "this entire world belongs to God" and that "adoration of him takes place not in Jerusalem alone but everywhere in spirit and truth."[20] In short, the individual act of worship gets its value from the larger basis and pool of meaning which is the liturgy of the world and of history. For the Christian imagination, Jesus Christ provides the centering moment in this extended liturgy that he represents and symbolizes; his cross and resurrection reflect the pattern of the liturgy of the world and history. Thus, the reversal is complete: Liturgy in the formal sense draws its strength and value from the dramatic liturgy of the world and history.

(iv) How exactly, then, do sacrament and liturgy work? They perform by symbolizing: by externalizing and making historically real and actual the inner dynamism of grace in human life. Instead of seeing sacraments as injecting God's presence and grace into people during a liturgical or sacramental celebration, which they in turn extend in life in the world, one should rather think of sacraments operating from outside-in: God acts within human subjects in their worldly encounters, and they bring that presence and action with them into the liturgical assembly. Grace comes into people's interior life through the world in the first instance: "[T]his grace is bestowed upon the world as such from its heart and center. It is constantly offered as the innermost finality of the world's history."[21] People then bring this to the liturgical service, where participation in sacraments and liturgy symbolize this inner reality—that is, expressing it outwardly. This gives the grace within the self a public expression by acting it out in representative actions, which in turn re-actualize the God-presence within the self and the worshiping community.

(v) In the end, Rahner affirms that the whole church should be a sacrament for the world. He suggests that this view of sacraments depicts what goes on in the church and in the world as a whole. The mission of the church in history is to be a community that is itself an effective sacrament witnessing to God's grace in the world. This suggests a concluding proposition on Christian ecclesial spirituality.

(vi) The mutuality and integral complementarity between everyday life and formal worship provide a foundational formula for drawing out a Christian spirituality of immersion in the world. But this simple formula is complicated by the spirituality of Johann Baptist Metz, and we now turn to his work.

A Brief Outline of Metz's Career as a Theologian. Metz was Rahner's student, one who became impressed by neo-Marxian conceptions of the social nature of human existence and a need to build that social dimension into a Rahnerian anthropology. In doing so, he developed distinctive dimensions of Christian spirituality that are his own but that, when joined to the transcendental theology of Rahner, give Christian spirituality a more adequate foundation.

Johann Baptist Metz was born in 1928. He grew up within the womb of the Bavarian Catholic Church. He described his small Catholic Bavarian town as late medieval in its distance from the modern world. As he became enculturated in modernity and the Enlightenment, he preserved the religious character of his roots as possessing dimensions that would protect modernity from self-destruction.[22] He also grew up during the Third Reich. "It is a richly textured fabric—woven from his rural Catholic upbringing, the ambiguous history of European Catholicism's relationship to modernity, the complicity or failure of German Catholicism under National Socialism, and his growing consciousness of the church's catholicity and the challenges deriving therefrom—that shapes his work."[23]

Metz tells a war story of an event that influenced his life and future career as a theologian. As a teenager and newly at the front, he was sent during the night as a messenger to headquarters. On his return the next day, he found that his unit had been wiped out. "This biographical background shines through all my theological work, even to this day. In it, for example, the category of memory plays a central role; my work does not want to let go of the apocalyptic metaphors of the history of faith, and it mistrusts an idealistically smoothed out eschatology. Above all, the whole of my theological work is attuned by a specific sensitivity for theodicy, the question of God in the face of the history of suffering in the world, in 'his' world."[24]

After the war, Metz was briefly imprisoned in the United States and learned English in the prison camp. On his return to Germany he began his course of studies leading to the priesthood. In the early 1950s he studied philosophy with Karl Rahner at Innsbruck and earned a doctorate in philosophy in 1952 with a work on Heidegger. He was ordained in 1954. In 1961, he was awarded a second doctorate in theology at Innsbruck, where he again worked with Rahner and wrote on Thomas Aquinas. From 1963 to 1993 he held a chair in fundamental theology at the University of Münster.[25] He was one of the co-founders of the post–Vatican II international journal of theology, *Concilium*, with Rahner, Hans Küng, and Edward Schillebeeckx in 1965.

Although Metz began his theological career as a Rahnerian, he gradually shifted his intellectual framework. After he took the position in fundamental theology at the University of Münster he read Horkheimer, Adorno, and Benjamin, who were part of the Frankfurt School of critical social thought. Walter Benjamin and Ernst Bloch helped Metz "to articulate the incipient apocalyptic sensibility that defines for him the 'mystical' element in Christianity."[26] He was also attentive to the Christian–Marxist dialogue that was taking place in Europe at the time. As Metz put it, the Christian–Marxist dialogue and members of the Frankfurt School "'politicized me out of' the existential and transcendental enchantment of theology."[27]

Metz came to realize that politics and political culture had to play a role in his thought about God. At the same time, political culture needed religion, for without it politics would yield to the dynamics of the survival of the fittest and the mighty would prevail and bury pluralism. Political freedom can survive only under transcendent ethical values. Metz also became preoccupied by a concern with human suffering. Theology has to be historically conscious, and thinking in terms of history has to confront historical catastrophes such as the Holocaust. This is theology's new dilemma: how to find a meaningful logic of history without jumping over or excluding these events.[28]

After retiring from Münster in 1993, Metz served as a visiting professor at the University of Vienna until 1997. He then returned to live in Münster until his death in 2019.[29]

Some Basic Concepts of Metz. Metz had a global outlook. New theological challenges were arising outside the West. As the influence of Western thinking lost some of its relevance, the voice of suffering around the world gained authority. Concern for social trauma outweighed the quest for logic and coherence. Intellectual credibility was relativized by a need for social moral credibility in the face of human suffering. Metz said that he respected and obeyed "the authority of those who suffer. For me this authority is the only one in which the authority of the sovereign God is manifested in the world for all men and women."[30] "The leitmotif of this biographical path is quite probably the *memoria passionis*, the remembrance of the suffering of others as a basic category of Christian discourse about God."[31]

The Text of Metz. We turn now to the text chosen to represent Metz and in some measure to complement Rahner.[32] In this essay, Metz contrasts his framework for theology with that of his mentor.[33] He proposes a theology from below, a critique of metaphysical and totalizing conceptions of history that he calls idealistic, and he sets in their place a narrative approach that entails an open metaphysics of process, incompletion, and a correlative epistemological reserve and humility. What follows is a map of his argument for a shift in perspective toward an explicitly social anthropology.

(i) Metz sets the stage for his proposal by noting that the main adversaries of a Christian vision in his day lay in Marxian and scientific evolutionary theories of history.

(ii) Theology has responded with two idealistic responses: One, inspired by Hegel, proposes a universal concept of history; the other turns to a transcendental conception of human existence as one finds in Karl Rahner.

(iii) Rahner's theory of anonymous Christianity symbolizes his approach.[34] All human beings are saved in Jesus Christ. The grace of salvation that God extends to all is the grace mediated by Jesus Christ. Thus the particular event of Jesus Christ is the cause of the salvation of all; this is recognized by Christians, while others participate in this salvation anonymously.

(iv) Metz appeals to a fable to illustrate the speculative character of Rahner's theological framework. Mr. and Mrs. Hedgehog, who look identical, stand at both ends of a racecourse, and thus it always appears that Mr. Hedgehog arrives ahead of Mr. Hare, who keeps going back and forth trying to win and runs himself to death.

(v) In the analogy with theology, the Hedgehog story represents Christian idealism that guarantees the integrity of history precisely by abstracting from actual events and postulating its outcome through a theology based on authority from above. It views the whole of history speculatively and idealistically. It stresses an abstract, objective salvation that is intended for all but is very distinct from the actual historical lives of people who are experiencing everything but being saved. It thus minimizes actual human suffering by absorbing it into a view that leaves the concrete human degradation of persons as the problem of individuals to be resolved existentially. The final salvation of the whole of history thus appears as already accomplished, while in fact it is merely postulated, independently of the actual tragedies of history.

(vi) By contrast, in Metz's case for a narrative practical Christianity, Mr. Hare represents historical Christianity. The hare runs the race. One has to look for the signs of salvation in actual history. Actual history is constituted by the lives of individuals and their sufferings. History as a process is an open narrative, a function of chance and freedom, so that its conclusion is not set. Its intelligibility now and in the future will be found in human praxis and the open promise of God. *Narrative* refers to the actual unfolding of events. Theology has to recall, narrate, and remember the histories of suffering, bear witness to revelation by a praxis of resisting human oppression and neglect, and hope for a salvation that incorporates this suffering into itself.

*   *   *

The theologies of Rahner and Metz are usually contrasted with each other, and there are several places where that contrast is legitimate. But it may be more fruitful to see these theologians not in the whole of their writings but in these texts, addressing the same world from two distinct perspectives, each of which sheds light on the dilemmas of life and the mystery of faith. The contrast thus becomes interactive and generative.

Notes

1. See R. Haight, A. Pach III, and A. Kaminski, eds., *Mysticism and Politics: Dietrich Bonhoeffer and Dorothee Soelle* (New York: Fordham University Press, forthcoming).

2. "Jesuits" is a short name for the members of the religious order of men formally known as the Society of Jesus. Since 1540 the order has been engaged in education and missionary activity and presently has members throughout the world.

3. Herbert Vorgrimler, *Karl Rahner: His Life, Thought and Works* (Glen Rock, NJ: Paulist Press, 1966), 20.

4. Interestingly, Rahner's thesis was not accepted by his director, who would accept only a strictly historical interpretation of Aquinas. The work was published in 1939 and remains a

foundational gateway to Rahner's thinking: *Spirit in the World*, trans. William Dych (New York: Herder and Herder, 1968).

5. Karl Rahner, *Hearer of the Word: Laying the Foundation for a Philosophy of Religion*, trans. Joseph Donceel (New York: Concilium, 1994).

6. Vorgrimler, *Karl Rahner*, 42.

7. The Second Vatican Council marked a turning point in Catholic theology; in the years following it, theologians accepted modernity to varying degrees and so began a movement of contextualization. In some respects, Rahner's work helped to anticipate and inspire the shift.

8. Several metaphors might be used to designate without elaboration the meaning of the Rahnerian term *unthematically*. It refers to the way something is perceived obliquely or not overtly but by implication. *Unthematically* thus means "not as an object," or not by a directly formulated clear or distinct idea. The point is to recognize how transcendent reality enters consciousness with a certain objectivity that goes beyond the limits of Kantian sensibility.

9. Karl Rahner, "Reflections on the Unity of the Love of Neighbor and the Love of God," in *Theological Investigations*, VI (Baltimore: Helicon Press, 1974), 231–49.

10. Ibid., 238.

11. Ibid., 239.

12. Ibid., 241.

13. Ibid.

14. Ibid., 243.

15. Ibid., 247..

16. Karl Rahner, "Considerations on the Active Role of the Person in the Sacramental Event," in *Theological Investigations*, XIV (New York: Seabury Press, 1976), 61–84.

17. Ibid., 166.

18. Ibid.

19. Ibid., 169.

20. Ibid.

21. Ibid., 178.

22. J. Matthew Ashley, "Introduction: Reading Metz," in Johann Baptist Metz, *A Passion for God: The Mystical–Political*

Dimension of Christianity, trans. J. M. Ashley (New York: Paulist Press, 1998), 10.

23. Ibid., 11.

24. Metz, "In Place of a Foreword: On the Biographical Itinerary of My Theology," in Ashley, *A Passion for God*, 2.

25. "In 1979 he was offered a prestigious position at the University of Munich, where Romano Guardini and then Rahner had taught earlier. But his appointment was vetoed by the then–Archbishop of Munich, Joseph Ratzinger (which led Rahner to write a fiery open letter in a German periodical: 'I Protest')." J. Matthew Ashley, "Remembering Johann Baptist Metz," *America* (December 3, 2019).

26. Ashley, "Introduction: Reading Metz," *A Passion for God*, 12.

27. Metz, "In Place of a Foreword," in Ashley, *A Passion for God*, 2. Here *existential* stands for a fixation on personal experience, in contrast to attention to context and the historical world of social suffering.

28. Ibid., 3–4.

29. Ashley, "Remembering."

30. Metz, "In Place of a Foreword," 4.

31. Ibid., 5.

32. The choice of this text was not motivated by a desire to set up a contrast between these two theologians, even though Metz sets up such a contrast. It is rather to illustrate how a spirituality that focuses on an individual's personal relationship with God opens up to a concern for social suffering. In fact, much of the social concern found in Metz in this period of his writing can also be found in Karl Rahner's later work. Moreover, after this essay, Metz went on to further differentiate his views from those of early Rahner. But the present volume is not a study in comparative spiritualities. It strives to show how the themes developed in the Rahner essays have to be carried into a socially conscious spirituality attentive to the theological aporias of relentless human suffering on a massive scale.

33. Johann Baptist Metz, "Transcendental-Idealist or Narrative-Practical Christianity? Theology and Christianity's Contemporary Identity Crisis," *Faith in History and Society: Toward a Practical*

Fundamental Theology, ed. J. Matthew Ashley (New York: Crossroad Publishing, 2007), 144–55.

34. The phrase "anonymous Christian" refers to the universality of God's saving grace, which was understood by Catholic theology at that time as constitutively mediated by Jesus Christ. That implied that all saving grace is the grace of Christ, making all who are saved "anonymously" Christian. The language has been criticized by many. The deeper question requires a theological discussion of religious pluralism which is not appropriate here.

II
The Texts

Karl Rahner: Reflections on the Unity of the Love of Neighbor and the Love of God[1]

Your Association has given itself a strangely adventurous and at the same time sacred task: it has the audacity to try to organize what cannot really be organized, to try to give to what is always new a permanent presence and to try to keep in the public eye what is hidden, what God alone sees and estimates. After all, it has only one real object—to love our neighbor in deed and in truth. You want to love by giving real help, but a help which is not merely an organized effort and effect of socio-political organization but which in truth remains love. Such love, however, where it truly exists and remains and *thus* really supports the social efforts between men—even though these efforts can also exist, be demanded and organized without real love—is not the function of secular society but itself constitutes a completely new society of men even where it has no name; it allows the eternal kingdom of God to begin in secret and is the miracle of the birth of eternity. Yet for this very reason this venture is strangely adventurous and daring. According to the Apostle, it is completely possible to give all one's goods to the poor and yet lack charity. This means surely that no matter how important and wonderful, and how "useful" socio-political action may be, it alone does not yet represent what is precisely the decisive factor of this undertaking; by this kind of action alone— without this mysterious love—your "Association" would sink to the level of a function of secular society and would become *that* which belongs to the age of a world which passes away. Hence, however much such love as is meant to govern here must think about how it can avoid the danger of becoming an empty feeling and nothing but talk and become a tangible helping action, we must also inquire here about what love is in itself. Even though we know basically what love is only by the fact that it takes place and thereby forgets to ask about itself, there is nevertheless—according to scripture—the Word, which commands it to act in God's name; hence there is also the responsible right to reflect about love itself, even though such reflection—unlike the commanding and promising word of love which goes out from the altar of the highest event of love, the cross—cannot bring with it the power of grace for that which is ultimately itself.

We intend to inquire into charity here by reflecting on its unity with the love of God. Precisely what is not meant, how-ever, is that charity loses itself in the depth of the love of God by dissolving itself or by becoming unimportant as such, or that two ways of fulfilling human existence, although each could be understood and carried out on its own, become subsequently associated. In the case of this unity the important thing is to understand rather that the one does not exist and cannot be understood or exercised without the other, and that two names have really to be given to the same reality if we are to summon up its one mystery, which cannot be abrogated.

Active Love as the Illuminating Situation of Modern Man's Existence

The question about the essential unity of love of God and neighbor which alone brings it about that the two

"commandments" are equal (Mt 22:39) and the realization
that on both together hang the Law and the Prophets (Mt
22:40) is more urgent today than ever before both for the
living action and the theoretical reflection which is carried by
that action and at the same time necessarily illumines it. To
get some idea of this urgency, we need only take a look at the
situation of contemporary philosophy. There is talk of the
end of metaphysics; it seems that, in some mysterious and
profound sense, we are also already questioning again the
transcendental philosophy of the pure subject, with its openness to the Absolute (in the form of the epoch-making conversion of the Greek cosmocentricity into a Christian, modern
anthropocentricity), whose meaning and also permanent
significance is only being slowly assimilated by Christian
philosophy and so will also no doubt be preserved by this in
its permanent meaning. Sociology is making an attempt to
replace metaphysics or to convert philosophy into an ontology
of intercommunication. The orientation of the philosophy of
cognoscitive transcendence toward a beyond which is always
valid seems to want to turn in the direction of hoped-for
future events; action is not now experienced as the derived
consequence of knowledge but rather knowledge is seen as
the event of self-consciousness which dwells only in action
itself. The God of the beyond of the world is suspected to be
a non-verifiable ghost which must be laid [aside], since he does
not exist there where we experience, achieve and suffer ourselves and where we suffer *ourselves* in solitude as the only
real bottomless abyss. One tries by thought and action to
demythologize everything and to destroy taboos in everything
until the only thing left is what seems to survive all this: the
incomprehensible something which is experienced as the
absurd something which one would like to honor by shocked
silence, or as the honest and bitter minimum of everyday duty
in the service of others, if one is still inclined to act on and
talk about an "ideal" at all.

Be that as it may, it must be placed over against the words
of the gospel and the liberating grace of the living God or

over against a sector which retains the courage not to despair and to withstand the impatient disappointment regarding every naturally always finite formula of human existence. Yet if Christianity is not to be merely "objectively" right but is also to say something right by its judgments to the man of *tomorrow* who must understand himself *where* and *in the manner* in which—after all—he exists, then it must obviously be made comprehensible to him that the *whole* truth of the gospel is still hidden and in germ in what he finds most easily as a deed and then as truth, viz. in the love of one's neighbor. If Christianity is faith, hope and charity, and if these three are not realities added to each other externally, each with a different origin and a different nature, but if love is rather the one word for the perfection of the one reality which we signify by these three names, then love could be the valid topical word for today which calls the whole of Christianity in the man of tomorrow into the concreteness of life and out of that depth into which God (and not ourselves) has immersed it by his offer of grace, the grace which he is himself. This presupposes, however, that it can really be said seriously that the love of God and the love of neighbor are one and the same thing, and that, in this way and in this way alone, we understand what God and his Christ are, and that we accomplish what is the love of God in Christ when we allow the love of our neighbor to attain its own nature and perfection.

Love of Neighbor Understood as Love of God: The Declarations of Scripture

The realization we are groping to reach, if we examine it honestly and soberly, is not as directly and clearly attested in scripture and tradition as one might think. They speak after all of two commandments (Mt 22:39; Mk 12:31), of the second of which it is said merely that it "resembles" the first. Nevertheless, the two together are valued in the Synoptic

tradition as the life-giving (Lk 10:28) epitome of the Old
Testament revelation in the scriptures and the prophets (Mt
22:40), greater than which there is nothing (Mk 12:31). Furthermore, in this Synoptic theology of love, it certainly must
not be overlooked that in the eschatological discourses about
the Judgment, love of neighbor is given in St. Matthew as the
only explicit standard by which man will be judged (Mt
25:34–46), and that the cooling down of this love is represented as the content of "lawlessness" among the afflictions
of the last days (Mt 24:12). In addition, there is that puzzling
saying in the Synoptic tradition that what is done to the least
of his brethren is done to Jesus, a saying which cannot be
explained by an arbitrarily altruistic identification which
according to many commentators Jesus himself undertakes
as it were merely morally and juridically in a mere "as if."
The understanding of this text must certainly first of all proceed from the absolutely unique position Jesus attributes to
himself as the Son as such, as the presence of God and of his
basileia among us, and must in general try to bring out clearly
the unity of this Son with man. If we do this, we will no doubt
be led back again to the doctrine of the mysterious unity of
the love of God and of neighbor and to its Christological
basis and radicalization. This doctrine becomes most radical
(though without any explicit reflection on this fact) in St. Paul:
love of neighbor (understood as the sovereign commandment:
Jn 2:8) is declared to be the fulfillment of *the* law (Rm 13:8,
10; Ga 5:14), and hence as the "bond" of perfection (Col
3:14) and as the better "way," i.e. as the Christian form of
existence simply and finally (1 Co 12:31–13:13). In St. John,
we find then a first reflection on the justification of this radical
elevation of the love of neighbor to being the totality of
Christian existence, a radical elevation which otherwise
might appear to be a pious exaggeration, as it is in fact
watered down in the reflective processes of the Christian
exhortation to virtue to the point that love of neighbor is a
single part of the Christian demand without which, in spite

of its difficulty, salvation is lost. According to St. John, we are loved by God (Jn 15:12) and by Christ so that we may love one another (Jn 13:34), a love which is the new commandment of Christ (Jn 13:34) which is his specifically (Jn 15:12) and which is the command imposed on us (Jn 15:17). Thus for St. John the consequence of this is that God who *is* Love (1 Jn 4:16) has loved us, not so that we might love him in return but so that we might love *one another* (1 Jn 4:7, 11). For we do not see God—he cannot be truly reached in gnostic-mystic interiority alone, in such a way that he would thus be really attainable by love (1 Jn 4:12)—and hence the "God in us" by mutual love is the God whom alone we can love (1 Jn 4:12), to such an extent that it is really true and that, although it is usually not at all clear to us, it is a radically convincing argument for St. John that "a man who does not love the brother whom he can see, cannot love God whom he has never seen" (1 Jn 4:20).

Many things remain undefined and unclear in the explicit wording of this attempt to make the concentration of the whole Christian relationship to God in the love of our neighbor comprehensible. Is perhaps even here the love of neighbor still merely the "proof" of our love of God simply because God, who is to be loved, has given us precisely this commandment to love our neighbor; and is, therefore, its fulfillment merely the best touchstone for us as to whether we are serious about the love of God, the whole matter resting ultimately nevertheless in two different partial fulfillments of Christian human existence and in two commandments? Is the word about the brother whom we see and about God whom we cannot see merely—after all—a simple *argumentum ad hominem*, an inference from the easier (which has not been achieved) to the more difficult (which will then certainly and a fortiori not be fulfilled)? Or may we take the words of St. John absolutely seriously, so that the "God in us" is really the one who alone can be loved and who is reached precisely in the love of our brother and in no other way, and that the love of neighbor encounters the love of God in *such* a way that it moves itself, and us with it, closer to the brother near by and attains both itself and the peak of perfection in the love of this brother, i.e. specifically as love of neighbor, and brings us to God and his love by the love of our neighbor?

Even though we cannot give a sure answer in the purely exegetical sense to this question of biblical theology, theological reflection in tradition gives us a little more courage to answer it in favor of the second part of the above alternative, i.e. in the direction of a radical identity of the two loves. It must be noted in this connection that while, on the one hand, even this theological tradition with its theologoumena does not give us any absolutely convincing solution to this problem yet, on the other hand, it does bring data of biblical theology[2] into play for our question which are not given their full effect in these texts or scripture itself which touch precisely on our question.

The Teaching of Theology

The tradition of the schools in Catholic theology has already held fast for a long time and this unanimously to the fact that the specific Christian love of neighbor is both in potency and in act a moment of the infused supernatural theological virtue of *caritas* by which we love God in his Spirit for his own sake and in direct community with him. This means, therefore, that the love of neighbor is not merely the preparation, effect, fruit and touchstone of the love of God but is itself an act of this love of God itself; in other words, it is at least an act within that total believing and hoping surrender of man to God which we call love and which alone justifies man, i.e. hands him over to God, because, being supported by the loving self-communication of God in the uncreated grace of the Holy Spirit, it really unites man with God, not as he is recognized by us but as he is in himself in his absolute divinity. Three things must not be overlooked in connection with this thesis of scholastic theology which identifies the love of God and neighbor at least in their supernatural potency of the one infused supernatural theological virtue of *caritas*. (1) Scholastic theology does *not* overlook (in principle quite correctly) the fact that such a *caritas* can be also a mere impulse for certain modes of relationship to others by personal love which are not themselves formally acts of charity but merely its *actus imperati* restricting themselves more to a merely human dimension. (2) Scholastic theology, when giving a more precise interpretation of its radical thesis, will presumably often fall short of it, especially when it tries to give reasons for it; it will realize this thesis and will give reasons for it in such a way that it really remains a thesis in words only, and it will not really catch up with the existential, ontological presuppositions of this thesis. (3) If scholastic theology were asked explicitly whether this identity is absolutely valid, it would no doubt answer that every act of charity toward our neighbor is indeed formally, even though perhaps only implicitly, love of God since the act is done after all by definition "for the sake of God loved with a supernatural love"; but scholastic theology would probably deny that conversely every act of the love of God is formally also a love of neighbor (even though it naturally includes also the *readiness* for this). Above all, most theologians today would still shrink from the proposition which gives our fundamental thesis its ultimate meaning, its real clarity and inescapable character, viz. that wherever a genuine love of man attains its proper nature and its moral absoluteness and depth, it is in addition always so underpinned and heightened by God's saving grace that it is also love of God, whether it be explicitly considered to be such a love by the subject or not.

Yet this is the direction in which the understanding of the thesis of identity as it is meant here leads us, since we hold it to be objectively correct and of basic significance for the Christian self-understanding of the future. What is meant by this requires a more detailed even though unavoidably still very summary explanation.

Love as a Reflected and Explicit Mode of Action and as an Unconceptualized Transcendental Horizon of Action

If we are to keep our ideas clear and avoid the most gross misunderstandings of the envisaged thesis from the very start, it is first of all necessary to distinguish in a human spiritual act between its explicit object represented in a determined concept and category, which is envisaged in a systematic way both by the intellect and will, on the one hand, and the *a priori* formal object, the transcendental horizon or "space" within which a determined individual object is encountered, on the other hand. The transcendental horizon is, on the one hand, the subjective possibility for the individual object to show itself at all; it is, as it were, the system of co-ordinates within which the classified object is given its place and which makes it comprehensible. On the other hand, the transcendental horizon is that which is itself given only in the encounter with the object of a concretely historical experience (it itself in transcendental experience), which of course does not mean that this experienced transcendental horizon of the categorized individual experience must be for this reason already systematically, explicitly and objectively represented and named. The latter is, of course, not usually the case. Indeed, even where this transcendental horizon of objective knowledge is reflected on and where it is therefore systematized, conceptually represented and named, and hence is itself made the explicit object of knowledge, this happens once more in virtue of this same horizon which as such must once more be given in an unconscious manner. The representation of its concept cannot dispense with this horizon itself in its unconscious exercise.

This distinction being presupposed, it must be said, of course, that not every act of the love of God is also a formal act of love of neighbor, if and in so far as the love of neighbor means an act in which our neighbor is envisaged and loved as the conscious object in its categorized and conceptual representation. If one relates oneself explicitly by prayer, trust and love to God, then this is in *this* sense an act of love of God and not an act of love of neighbor. Moreover, measured by the object, such an act of love of God has, of course, a higher dignity than an act of reflected love of neighbor. Yet where the whole "transcendental" depth of interhuman love is realized and represented (which, as has been said, *can* at least be *caritas*, as is quite certain from tradition), there such a love is also necessarily a conscious love of God and has God as its reflex motive (even though this is of course true once more in very different degrees of clarity). In this case our neighbor, and he himself, must then also be really loved and must be the formal object and motive of this love, no matter how one may explain the unity of the two then given motives. (The neighbor, through God's love for him, is "one" with God, etc.) Yet this still leaves open the other question which also occupies us here, viz. whether all interhuman love, provided only that it has its own moral radicality, is also *caritas* (i.e. love also of God), since it is orientated toward God, not indeed by an explicitly categorized motive but (and this is the question) by its inescapably given transcendental horizon, which is given gratuitously by God's always prevenient saving grace.

The Anonymous "Christianity" of Every Positively Moral Activity

A second preliminary remark must therefore be made: we presuppose here in what follows a theological opinion[3] which is not indeed commonly held in Catholic theology but which has a sufficiently serious basis to allow it to be presupposed here, even though it is impossible here to develop this basis. This opinion states that wherever man posits a positively moral act in the full exercise of his free self-disposal, this act is a positive supernatural salvific act in the actual economy of salvation even when its *a posteriori* object and the explicitly given *a posteriori* motive do not spring tangibly from the positive revelation of God's Word but are in this sense "natural." This is so because God in virtue of his universal salvific will offers everyone his supernaturally divinizing grace and thus elevates the positively moral act of man. Furthermore, the thereby already given, supernaturally transcendental even though unconscious horizon of the spirit (its *a priori* orientation toward the triune God of eternal life) includes an element of (transcendental) revelation and possibility of faith which also gives such an act that sufficient character of "faith" necessary for a moral act being a salvific act. This opinion states, therefore, that wherever there is an absolutely moral commitment of a positive kind in the world and within the present economy of salvation, there takes place also a saving event, faith, hope and charity, an act of divinising grace, and thus *caritas* is exercised in this, a fact which still remained an open question above. There is a possible logical but not a real distinction between a moral act and a salvific act. Yet all this does not mean that we have proved our proper basic thesis about the strict mutual identity of the love of God and the love of neighbor. It still remains questionable whether such love of neighbor is just *any* one of the moral acts among many others of equal rank which we must interpret as saving acts, or whether this love has a special, all-embracing position within the whole of morality, in such a way that it must be taken as the basis and sum total of the moral as such and hence—when divinized by grace—can be regarded as *the* saving act of explicit love of God in the sense that even conversely every act of explicit love of God is truly and formally (though in a sense still to be determined more exactly) love of *neighbor*.

Love of Neighbor as the Basic Moral Activity of Man

It is the second part of this alternative which must be affirmed. Love of neighbor, even and especially if we regard it to begin with as a *moral* phenomenon and do not yet ask about the theological virtue of charity at all, is not to begin with just any of the many co-existing morally right reactions of man toward his own reality and that of his surroundings, but is the basis and sum total of the moral as such. Why and in what sense is this so? In the external multiplicity of his surroundings, man encounters at a first glance a colorful, apparently arbitrary, juxtaposed variety of objects toward which his moral activity too can be referred in each case and which—as is shown, for instance, by the systematizations of special ethics—are then subsequently and somewhat arbitrarily collected together and ordered in groups. Yet still, the world encountered by man (we prescind from God at this point) is in many respects more originally *one* world of man. This is already seen to be true by the fact that the true and proper surrounding of man is his personal environment. This environment of persons is the world through which man finds and fulfills himself (by knowledge and will) and . . . gets away from himself. From a personal and moral point of view, the world of things is of significance only as a factor for man and for his neighbor. This follows first of all from the *a priori* structure of the one whole man (in knowledge and will), a structure which imposes a unified law of its possible knowledge on the external variety of possible objects and which thus systematizes this variety as it is known and willed. Knowledge is, however, of its nature a "being-within-oneself," or rather a return to one*self*, and freedom is not simply the capacity to do this or that but (formally) a *self*-disposing into finality; the subject (from a formal point of view) is always concerned with itself. Hence it must necessarily be the secret *a priori* law imposed on the multiplicity of the possible objects for man that they can be concerned with and be ordered for man's knowledge and freedom, precisely in so far as they can serve this "being-within-*oneself*" and this self-disposal. It follows from this, however, that the world of things can be a possible object for man's concern only as a moment of the world of persons. In the traditional teaching this is seen also in the axiom: being and the good are identical; the objective *moral* good is given in a *personal* being; thus a good which is not the person or something referred to the person as such cannot be regarded as an objective value of moral action. Nevertheless it must be added immediately that this formal nature of knowledge and freedom, understood as self-possession and self-deed, refers to the *formal* nature from a certain point of view and must not be misunderstood in an egocentric sense. Materially—even merely on account of the mundaneness and *a posteriori* historicity of man—the *a posteriori* object is the necessary mediation of the knowing subject to itself and so, presupposing what has just been said, the known personal Thou is the mediation, the "being-within-oneself" of the subject. This condition is even clearer and more radical in the case of freedom: the free self-disposal, when morally right and perfect, is precisely the loving communication with the human *Thou* as such (not as mere negation of nor as something different from the "ego" which wants merely to find *itself*, even though in the other). Yet since knowledge (being itself already an act) attains its proper and full nature only in the act of freedom and therefore must lose and yet keep itself in freedom in order to be completely itself, it has a fully human significance only once it is integrated into freedom, i.e. into the loving communication with the Thou. The act of personal love for another human being is therefore the all-embracing basic act of man which gives meaning, direction and measure to everything else. If this is correct, then the essential *a priori* openness to the other human being which must be undertaken freely belongs as such to the *a priori* and most basic constitution of man and is an essential inner moment of his (knowing and willing) transcendentality. This *a priori* basic constitution (which must be accepted in freedom, but to which man can also close himself) is experienced in the concrete encounter with man in the concrete. The one moral (or immoral) basic act in which man comes to himself and decides basically about himself is also the (loving or hating) communication with the concrete Thou in which man experiences, accepts or denies his basic *a priori* reference to the Thou as such. Everything else is a factor in this or a consequence of it or an impulse toward it, but in the present order of salvation, i.e. one having a supernatural goal, *this basic* act is, according to what has been said, elevated supernaturally by a self-communication of God in uncreated grace and in the resulting basic triune faculty of the theological virtues of faith, hope and charity, whereby theological love necessarily and of its very nature integrates and saves faith and hope into itself. Hence the one basic human act, where it takes place positively, is the love of neighbor understood as *caritas*, i.e. as a love of neighbor whose movement is directed toward the God of eternal life.

Love of Neighbor as Man's Manifestation of His Wholeness and Essence

The reduction of the spiritual knowing and willing reality of man to that love of his neighbor which is *caritas*, when seen as man's basic act, does not of course limit this act to the obviously and transparently ordinary everyday events but, even if we prescind to begin with from its theological aspect, gives this act a quality of mystery. When we say that a self-understanding of man—understood as the assembling of his knowledge and as the free self-determination of man with a view to finality—takes place in the act of loving communication with the Thou (in this and in nothing else) so that everything else is a moment, presupposition, initial stage or result of *this*, then we also say of course *eo ipso* and conversely that the whole incalculable mystery of man is contained and exercised in this act of love of neighbor; it means that *all* anthropological statements must also be read as statements about that love which is not merely a "regional" happening in the life of man but is the whole of himself in which alone he possesses himself completely, meets himself completely and falls into the ultimate abyss of his nature.

His corporeality, his temporality and historicity, his final incapacity to catch up with himself by reflection, the unfathomable and adventurous character of his existence, the anticipation of his future in hope or despair, the bitter impossibility of his perfecting and fulfilling himself and the disillusion proper to him, his continual confrontation with the nameless, silent, absolute mystery which embraces his existence, his readiness for death which after all can also be seen—in a very peculiar way—as the basic act of existence ... all these together are necessarily also the essential traits of *love* for another person. The love of neighbor is not something which everyone always already knows reflexly in the depth of his being; rather, it is that which is sent to man only through the experienced and suffered wholeness of life and still remains even then, indeed especially then, a nameless mystery. It would be necessary to show by an empirical and descriptive phenomenology of love, responsibility, loyalty, venture, and of the unfinished and eternal quality inherent in love what breadths and depths are implied by love of the Thou, how man really experiences in it who he is, how the "no" to it imprisons the *whole* man within the deadly lonely damnation of self-created absurdity, how the totality of reality, which freely gives itself and is accepted and understood as the blessed incomprehensibility—which is the only self-evident thing— opens itself only if man opens himself radically in the act of love and entrusts himself to this totality. It would be necessary to show more empirically than is possible here what is the mutual relation of dependence between the transcendental openness and readiness for unlimited communication with the Thou, on the one hand, and the concrete encounter with the concrete Thou, on the other hand. This would make it more comprehensible that in the act of love for another, and in it alone and primarily, the original unity of what is human and what is the totality of man's experience is collected together and achieved, and that the love for the other concrete Thou is not just something which also exists in man among many other things but is man himself in his total achievement.

If it would thus become clearer by the description of love of the other Thou that this love is really the fulfillment of the total and hence also spiritually transcendental nature of man, then it would also become easier to grasp that it occurs in the present economy of salvation only in the form of *caritas*, for *caritas* means nothing else than the absolute radicality of this love in so far as it is open to the immediacy of the God who communicates himself under the form of grace.

Normally speaking, we merely say quite abstractly in our teaching on grace that the absolute, infinite transcendentality of the spirit is the *potentia oboedientialis* for grace and that it is liberated by grace—in its infinity which of itself belongs to this transcendentality—from being the *mere* condition of the possibility of grasping a certain categorized object to being the possibility of immediate presence to God as he is in himself. This declaration, however, would have to be made concrete in the knowledge that from a more concrete point of view this *potentia oboedientialis* is precisely the transcendentality toward the other who is to be loved and who first of all is one's fellow man. Even by theological reflection we must arrive at the point where we can say: if in the present economy of salvation and on account of the universal salvific will of God *every* radically free moral act becomes a saving act through grace and is thus orientated toward the immediate presence to God (as has already been said), then this must be true *a fortiori* of the basic moral act which integrates everything, viz. the love of our neighbor. Even though this, the supernatural nature of a saving act, cannot be grasped reflexly

by an arbitrary introspection alone[4] (but this is to be ascribed
to that systematization into themes which takes place precisely
in man's history of salvation and revelation), it would nevertheless be possible to show, by such a phenomenological
description of the empirical, authentic love of neighbor, the
elements in it which are elevated and liberated by grace to
their absolute perfection and which are then also experienced
as such unsystematically. Furthermore, it is not the place here
to describe the different concrete forms of love of neighbor.
Suffice it to say explicitly here that, even when we are talking
about *caritas*, it must always be a question of real love and
that it is therefore not just a matter of fulfilling a commandment which guards and defends the other against our brutal
egoism; "love for God's sake"—to be precise—does not mean
love of God alone in the "material" of our neighbor merely
seen as an opportunity for pure love of God, but really means
the love of our neighbor himself, a love empowered by God
to attain its ultimate radicality and a love which really termi-
nates and rests in our neighbor.

The Encounter of the World and of Man as the Medium of the Original, Unobjectified Experience of God

We must now finally give thought to an objection against any
thesis which understands the love of neighbor as the one all-
embracing basic act of human existence, viz. that the *religious*
act directed toward God is the basic act of human existence
or at least stands equally entitled and equally original, indeed
with higher rank, beside the act of loving communication
with another person. This objection is, however, a misunderstanding. It must be noted first of all that, at least for the
original experience of God, God is not one "object" besides
others either objectively speaking or in the subjective intentionality of man (in knowledge and free action and their
unity). God is not an object toward which the intentionality

of man can be directed in the same fragmentary and particular
way as it is toward the multiplicity of objects and persons
encountered within the categories of intramundane experience. God is not originally given in the way in which—as if
by chance, externally and without it having to be thus by the
nature of human intentionality—a flower or Australia is
"given." We must not consider man as unconcerned about
God until he systematically conceives the notion of God as
one reality "besides" others and this in the merely dividing
distinction from these other realities. In the original act which
precedes all reflex systematizations, God is always given as
the subjectively and objectively all-bearing *ground* of experience, a ground which is beyond this world; he is therefore
given indirectly in a kind of boundary experience as the origin
and destination of an act which is objectively directed toward
the world and which, therefore, as will have to be said in more
detail below, is a loving communication with (or "no" to) the
Thou in the world. God is primarily and originally given in
(or as) the transcendental, unclassified horizon of the knowing
and acting intentionality of man and not as an "object"
represented by an idea within this horizon. Moreover, even
where God is made the subject of religious and Christian
reflection—hence, where and in so far as (over and above such
a philosophico-religious reflection) he is given (transcendentally) in the "horizon" of the spirit opened up or maintained
in its absolute manner by divinizing grace (as the goal of
this transcendentality which transmits itself supernaturally)
and where he speaks himself (in categories) through the
revelation of the Word in salvation history, and where in
both these ways he becomes a "partner" in a personal and
direct relationship between himself and man—this revelation
of grace and the Word and the real self-communication by
grace always happens *vis-à-vis* and through man who is
already "in the world," i.e. who is given to himself in freedom
by entering in love into the world around him, and by

personal encounter and communication with the Thou of intramundane experience.

The (naturally and supernaturally) transcendental experience of God which is also the necessary presupposition of the historical revelation of the Word and both is and remains its supporting ground is possible only in and through man, who has *already* (in logical priority) experienced the human Thou by his intramundane transcendental experience (of his *a priori* reference to the Thou) and by his categorized experience (of his concrete encounter with the concrete Thou) and who only *in this way* can exercise the (at least) transcendental experience of his reference to the absolute mystery (i.e. God). The classical thesis of scholastic theology (against ontologism and the innate idea of God) which maintains that God can be known only *a posteriori* from the created world does not ultimately mean to imply (if it is properly understood) that man merely comes upon God like any object given to him purely accidentally (e.g. this flower or Australia) with which he might just as well not be concerned (from the point of view of the *a priori* structure of his knowledge) but it does mean that the transcendentally original *a priori* experience of his original reference to God and thus of God himself (an experience which must in some measure also be objectified in categories) can be made only in an always already achieved going-out into the world which, understood as the world of man, is primarily the people *with whom* he lives. Precisely because the original reference toward God is of a transcendental kind and hence does not fall into any category but is given in the infinite reference of the spirit of man beyond every mere object of his personal and material surroundings, the *original* experience of God (as distinct from his separating representation in an individual concept) is always given in a "worldly" experience. This, however, is present only originally and totally in the communication with a "Thou."

Since every conceptual reflection on the transcendental conditions of the possibility of knowledge and freedom is itself based once more on these same conditions, then even the *explicit* religious act in which God becomes the reflex theme of knowledge and love is once more underpinned and taken up by that act which offers a transcendental, inclusive experience of God (of a natural–supernatural kind) and this *by the fact* that this act—in our turning toward the people we live with, and therefore in our explicit communication with them—lets us also experience unreflectedly the transcendental conditions of this act (i.e. the transcendental reference to God and the transcendental openness to the human Thou).

The act of love of neighbor is, therefore, the only categorized and original act in which man attains the whole of reality given to us in categories, with regard to which he fulfills himself perfectly correctly and *in which* he always already makes the transcendental and direct experience of God by grace. The reflected religious act *as such* is and remains secondary in comparison with this. It has indeed, as has already been said, a higher dignity than the reflected act of love of neighbor, if and in so far as the latter is measured by the particular explicit, conceptually represented object of the act in question. Measured by its "horizon" or its transcendental possibility, it has the same dignity, the same "draught" and the same radicality as the act of explicit love of neighbor, since both acts are necessarily supported by the (experienced but unreflected) reference both to God and to the intramundane Thou and this by grace (of the infused *caritas*), i.e. by that on which the explicit acts both of our relationship to God and of our love of neighbor "for God's sake" reflect. Yet this does not alter the fact that the primary basic act of man who is always already "in the world" is always an act of the love of his neighbor and *in this* the original love of God is realized in so far as in this basic act are also accepted the conditions of its possibility, one of which is the reference of man to God when supernaturally elevated by grace.

Love of Neighbor as the Primary Act of Love of God

We are now in a position to give a direct answer to the basic question of our whole reflections. This was the question about the identity of the love of God and the love of neighbor. More exactly, it was the question about whether the love of neighbor understood as *caritas* is ultimately only a secondary moral act (one among many) which more or less proceeds objectively from the love of God as an *actus imperatus*. In other words, does the love of neighbor have God for its "motive" (just as in the explicit love of God) in such a way that this love of neighbor really "loves" God alone and hence, in accordance with the will of God who is really loved, is well disposed toward its neighbor and does good to him? *Or* is there a more radical unity between the love of God and of neighbor (taken as *caritas*) in such a way that the love of God itself is always also already love of neighbor in which our neighbor is really loved himself? We can now answer: the categorized explicit love of neighbor is the primary act of the love of God. The love of God unreflectedly but really and always intends God in supernatural transcendentality in the love of neighbor as such, and even the explicit love of God is still borne by that opening in trusting love to the whole of reality which takes place in the love of neighbor. It is radically true, i.e. by an ontological and not merely "moral" or psychological necessity, that whoever does not love the brother whom he "sees" also cannot love God whom he does not see, and that one can love God whom one does not see only *by* loving one's visible brother lovingly.

Finally, we would simply draw the reader's attention to the fact that we should really go on to reflect now explicitly on the "Christological" and "eschatological" aspects of this situation. If in "recent times" (and only then) one has learned to see and love the Father whom one does not see in the man Jesus whom one does see, then the unity of the love of God and of neighbor on which we have been reflecting becomes even more radical from a Christological and eschatological point of view and thus reaches its climax; thus the man Jesus takes on and continues to have an eternal significance for our relationship to God right into the "direct" vision of God.

The relationship to God through man is thus not merely a "mediation" in time but also in eternity, and therefore the same is present "subjectively" as is present "objectively" through the never reversed acceptance of humanity by the Logos. Unfortunately we cannot enter further into this here, otherwise it could also be shown how a love of neighbor which has reached an absolute (supernatural) perfection of being also includes Christology.

The Topical Significance of the Love of Neighbor for Modern Man's Knowledge of God

This whole laborious reflection may appear as if it only considers something which, if true, is valid *always* and everywhere (at least in the Christian order of salvation). This is quite correct yet our reflections have particular significance for the historical "moment" in which we live *today*. A natural–supernatural knowledge and love of God of an existentially authentic kind, in which the reality of God is truly experienced, is in the very nature of things an act which can only be posited by man as *a whole*. Everything he is and with which he is concerned must be included in this, otherwise the absolute ground of reality, the ground of the knowing and acting spirit, would not be encountered in it and God would not appear in it as God, as a Person, as Freedom and as absolute mystery. This reality, however, which achieves itself as a whole toward God, has nevertheless different aspects in different periods for the man who fulfills himself historically, privileged aspects under which it presents itself and transmits itself to man. Each epoch has different "catchwords," "primitive words," under which the one totality of the experience of God is summoned up and comes toward us anew out of the totality of our experience of reality and of ourselves.

Already in scripture, and then also in the course of the history of faith and salvation, there shows itself a variety of such catchwords which always mean and imply the whole and yet appear at the same time as many *different* gateways which form *the* particular approach to this whole according to the spirit of each particular age or as particular characteristics of the Christian religious experience of particular men. For St. Paul, for instance, the "catchword" is *faith*, but this is not the same for everyone or every age, even though no one can come to God without faith. It could be asked whether the trilogy of the three divine virtues does not *also* already indicate a sphere of such a change of "root terms" for a religious experience in a particular period, just as the key-word for everything in St. John is not faith but love, while the Synoptics replace even this by "conversion" (*metanoia*). Today, at any rate, when by reason of its enormous numbers, its concrete unity and in its necessarily new social forms, mankind must learn to love completely anew or go under; when God opens out anew as the silent incomprehensibility so much so that man is tempted to honor him now simply by silence and nothing else and when all atheism, which today really exists for the first time, is simply the mistaken adolescent form of this opportunity and the temptation given to us as regards God's incomprehensibility; when an extremely worldly world is coming into being, a world which man creates for himself and which ought not indeed be sacralized but which must be experienced and acted in the depth *sanctified* by God, i.e. opened toward him ... at the dawn of such a new epoch, "love of neighbor" might easily be the root-word which really moves people and the key-word for today. Nevertheless, if we want to say today that anyone who loves his neighbor has fulfilled *the* law as such—namely that if we love one another, then God's final salvation is within us (as one might translate

1 Jn 4:12)—then we must understand absolutely fundamentally why the love of neighbor, provided it is genuine and
accepts its own proper incomprehensible being to the very
limit, already contains the whole of Christian salvation and
of Christianity. This must indeed still be unfolded in that
complete fullness and breadth which we know and preserve,
but whenever someone loves someone else truly and "to the
end," it is already grasped in its original root.

Notes

1. In this essay, the author takes up in greater detail and
more exactly reflections which he has used for the question of
the veneration of the Saints (cf. *GuL* XXXVII [1964], pp.
325-40, on the question of possibility). Cf. also K. Rahner, "The
'Commandment' of Love in relation to the other Commandments,"
Theological Investigations V (London & Baltimore, 1966), 439-59.

2. For example, when scripture declares that the love of
neighbor is supported by the same *pneuma* (Ga 5:22).

3. Cf. on this, e.g., K. Riesenhuber, "Der anonyme Christ nach
K. Rahner," *ZKT* LXXXVI (1964), 286-303; A. Röper, *Die
anonymen Christen* (Mainz 1963); K. Rahner, *Zur Theologie des
Todes* (Freiburg, 1963), 79-86 (English translation: *On the
Theology of Death*, Quaestiones Disputatae 2 [Freiburg &
Edinburgh–London, 1961]—*Tr.*).

4. The supernatural character of the saving act is also not
simply what is beyond consciousness, as is held by a nominalistic
tendency in theology even to our own day (outside the Thomistic
school). Cf. on this K. Rahner, "Gnadenerfahrung," *LTK* IV, pp.
1001 *sq.*; K. Rahner, *Theological Investigations* III (London &
Baltimore, 1967), 86-90; J. Alfaro, *LTK* IV, 207 *sq.*

Karl Rahner: Considerations on the Active Role of the Person in the Sacramental Event

In the considerations which follow we shall be examining the active role of the person in the conferring of the sacraments. We shall, of course, be including within our purview all those sacraments in which the full consciousness and living faith of the subject is engaged in his act of receiving them. In practice, therefore, only infant baptism will remain outside the scope of our present considerations. However, since the theme is so broad in scope, we shall concentrate chiefly on the Eucharist. Here the distinction between the sacrificial act and the reception of the sacrament will be left in the background. Yet for our present purposes the Eucharist is taken as representative of all the sacraments. One who is theologically educated can easily apply our statements about the Eucharist and the points which apply first and foremost to it to the other sacraments, each according to its special character, and there is no necessity to provide a special exposition of this in each particular case. While, therefore, we are treating explicitly of the Eucharist, our remarks are intended to apply to all the sacraments.

We have set ourselves to state, to justify, and to elucidate certain principles, and to show them to be orthodox in terms

of dogmatic theology. This implies something like an application of a Copernican approach[1] to the general conception
of the sacraments, consisting in an intellectual and spiritual
movement of the sacramental event outward to take effect in
the "world," and backward in a spiritual movement leading
from the world to the sacrament. This way of putting it may
sound somewhat grandiose, and is presumably still not wholly
comprehensible. The whole of the considerations which follow
are intended to contribute toward an elucidation of this initial
statement. Only so can the religious significance of this "Copernican application" effectively be rendered intelligible. In
this connection we are of course aware that in order to clarify
our special concern we must in some respects simplify, and
must separate and draw contrasts between realities which in
concrete life always exist in unison, albeit in varying propor-
tions and with some more apparent than others.

The Old Model: Sacrament as Isolated Encounter with God

How does the average Catholic Christian feel about a sacrament as he customarily receives it? We might describe this act
of receiving (though of course with the provisos already
mentioned) as follows: the Christian feels that he lives in a
secular world. He is aware that his life in this world is subject
to commandments of God which are difficult to fulfill. He is
aware of being summoned by God and set upon a course
which leads him out of this present life through the gates of
death and beyond into the eternity of God. He has to maintain
union with God, his true future and the law-giver presiding
over his life even in the present. He passes to and fro from
this secular world into a sacral sphere a "fanum" or "temple."
It is only here (and in a true sense exclusively here, so far as
his personal feelings are concerned, whatever his head may
tell him from its stock of theological knowledge) that it is

possible to achieve any real encounter with God in which this God meets him not merely as making moral demands upon him but as sanctifying him and bestowing grace and strength upon him. This is achieved precisely in the sacraments and above all by holy Mass in the Eucharist. In these sacraments God's actions upon humanity touch the individual as it were from without, penetrate him, sanctify him, and transform him (at least carrying these processes a stage further, although for the most part the effects are experienced as very transitory and in a sense peripheral). Here man encounters God and Jesus the Lord so that afterward he can (ideally speaking) be sent by him to go forth once more into a secular world, there to pursue his monotonous everyday duties in a certain sense remote from God. Here in the sacrament (as in no other circumstances) man achieves closeness and union with God. Here he has left the secular world behind him. Here, and in a true sense here alone, that takes place which renders life meaningful and "religious" (i.e. united to God).

In the achievement of Christian living is such a viewpoint really the only possible one in the light of our understanding of the Christian faith—a viewpoint in which the sacramental event constitutes the true apogee of Christian living? This can be doubted and indeed denied. But in denying it we are not rejecting the legitimacy of this common conceptual model of the place which the Eucharist and the sacraments have in general in our lives. What we are rejecting, rather, is the idea that we are compelled to accept this viewpoint as the only possible one. We can also "experience" the sacraments in a quite different way.

We may begin by stating quite freely that the earlier conceptual model we have described is nowadays much under attack. Modern man's awareness of reality is such (it makes no difference whether this in itself should be subjected to critical questioning or whether it is anything but an absolute norm) that the sacraments as taken in this sense are all too easily thought of as religious rites which bypass the dimension of "real reality" or "real life." The sacraments fall under the suspicion of being empty ritualism, so that it is only in terms of an ideology which is nowadays difficult to achieve or to maintain that they can be felt as important or as an effective force in human life. In this conceptual model we all too easily receive the impression that the sacraments, the Mass, are "useless," that they are incapable of bringing about any real effects in human life, that after Mass everything goes on as before and as it would go on even without Mass. If the "religious man" attributes "consolation" and strengthening to his religious experiences, which after all he undergoes in receiving the sacraments, then the less "religious" man will reflect that the other is fleeing from the harsh realities of life into an ideological world of unreality, albeit one of a psychic unburdening, and that this world of unreality on the one hand does nothing to alter the "realities" of life while on the other it endures only so long as we fail to see through the psychic mechanisms and techniques involved in such "consolation." And if we are then called upon to "take out with us into our everyday life" the sacrifice of Christ, to let the sacraments take effect in our lives, then this is merely to set up a moral norm and obligation the powerlessness of which is something from which it is sought to flee precisely through the sacraments. For (on this view) it is not the sacraments which carry the individual out into life by their power, but rather the individual himself who must carry them out into life by his own new moral strivings to meet and so to fulfill the claims of morality which they make upon him. That which we experience as their power is in reality the special new moral striving which we regard as required of us in order to fulfill their ideals. More acutely than in former times we have the feeling that the numerical frequency of our reception of the sacraments does not *ipso facto* have any true religious significance (even when it is undertaken with good will) unless we regard the reception of the sacraments as being itself in turn a "good work," the value of which increases *ipso facto* according to the number of times it is repeated, in which case we are running counter to the intrinsic meaning of the sacraments themselves.[2] The present-day tendencies, even within the Catholic sphere, toward a "desacralization" of Christianity and of Christian living may in many respects be false or questionable. But in any case they do produce unease with regard to sacral and sacramental activities. With regard to the statement of the Second Vatican Council that the Mass constitutes the supreme point of Christian living it may be doubted whether, even if we confine ourselves to serious Christians only, this *ipso facto* expresses their real attitude of mind.[3]

It is not only fashionable tendencies toward "secularization" of one kind or another that nowadays represent a threat to the free use of the sacraments. A far more basic danger is represented by that recognition, which is nowadays becoming clearer, of the difference between a genuine and authentic achievement of human living on the one hand and our conceptual models of, and reflections upon it at a secondary level on the other. What do we mean by this? If, for instance, someone prays: "O God I will love you with my whole heart. This is my conscious, free, and unconditional decision," then surely everyone will admit that even in any genuine and well-intentioned declaration (in prayer etc.) of this kind the individual concerned is still far from really loving God "with his whole heart." By a process of objectification he has, in his own conscious reflections, constructed a conceptual or verbal model of a whole-hearted love of this kind, and has also in some sense affirmed it. But this replica of whole-hearted love is not the whole-hearted love itself. For this latter (if it is present at all) is achieved at a more basic level seeing that freedom is more basic than the reflective concept of it by which we name it (even when we may be seeking to achieve it). A further point is that even at its more basic level freedom is far from being empowered at every moment of the individual's personal history to achieve that toward which it is of its very nature orientated: radically to control the total and ultimate reality of the person in all dimensions in such a way as to determine its final and irrevocable state. Now of their very nature the acts in which we receive the sacraments are attempts, as a matter of the radical decision of our freedom, in a spirit of love and from our whole hearts to orientate ourselves irrevocably to God. Yet precisely in the light of his experience of the nature of freedom, which always remains ultimately beyond the scope of any conscious manipulation on the part of the subject, modern man feels himself beset by problems in his reception of the sacraments precisely when this takes place very frequently and without any special reference to the unfolding process of freedom in the true sense and the *kairos* it contains, which it is not given to the subject to decide upon at will. Modern man all too easily has the impression of acting ungenuinely and even dishonestly, and precisely in those cases in which this reception of the sacraments is related excessively and exclusively from the outset to the individual's own personal saving history taken in isolation. For in this act of receiving the sacraments it is not always possible for something particularly decisive to take place such as can be readily brought to fruition through the ritual celebration of a sacrament. Evidently such problems are not fully disposed of by that factor which we are seeking to treat of here, namely the broadening of the awareness of the recipient of the sacraments so as to view saving history within world history as a whole or by relating them in faith to that grace which constitutes the dynamic force and the *entelecheia* of this whole saving history, drawing the individual man into this history and shaping its own manifestation in the sacramental sign within the individual life. Nevertheless these problems are diminished and made easier to solve if the recipient of the sacrament is conscious from the outset of being drawn into this "cosmic" history of grace.

A New Model: Using the Whole of Life to Bring the Sacrament to Its Fullness

But is there another view of the Eucharist and of the sacraments? Yes there is. It is based upon the simple fact of dogmatics that that which we call sanctifying grace and divine
life is present *everywhere* where the individual does not close
himself to God who creates salvation by a real and culpable
denial, and further on the fact that in a real sense, albeit to
some extent unconsciously, this grace is brought about and
made manifest in the concrete conditions of history and of
human life wherever men live and die so long as this life of
theirs has not come to imply mortal guilt. We have no intention here of developing, justifying, or defending this fact of
dogmatics in any greater detail here.[4] All that we shall do is
to elucidate it in its further implications for an understanding
of the sacraments that either has been, or is to be transformed,
and that too as concretely as possible.

God's Grace as Creating Salvation at the Roots of Human Existence

The world is permeated by the grace of God. The sacraments
are specific events of God's grace as forgiving, sanctifying,
and imparting the divine nature. But while they have this
significance this does not mean that it is solely in the moment
of the sacramental act that the grace of God impinges upon
a world that is secular and devoid of grace as from without,
as though it sought to penetrate this world and, in the very
act of so seeking, gradually lost its pristine force and receded
until a fresh act of the same kind renewed it once more. The
world is constantly and ceaselessly possessed by grace from
its innermost roots, from the innermost personal center of
the spiritual subject. It is constantly and ceaselessly sustained

and moved by God's self-bestowal even prior to the question (admittedly always crucial) of how creaturely freedom reacts to this "engracing" of the world and of the spiritual creature as already given and "offered," the question, in other words, of whether this creaturely freedom accepts the grace to its salvation or closes itself to it to its perdition. Whether the world gives the impression, so far as our superficial everyday experience is concerned, of being imbued with grace in this way, or whether it constantly seems to give the lie to this state of being permeated by God's grace which it has, this in no sense alters the fact that it is so. And without this belief and hope that the world has been endowed with grace in precisely *this* sense, the appeal to the sacraments as almost intermittent moments when such "engracing" takes place would seem to modern man unworthy of belief. He would be unable to avoid the impression that what is involved in the doctrine of the sacraments is an ideological elevation of a world that is hideously secular, and one which conceals the truth without really changing the world itself.

At the present moment the time is not ripe to enquire what meaning the sacraments can then have, if they are not to be thought of as the particular moments in which God "intervenes" in his world from without. If we say that grace has all along possessed reality from the innermost heart and center of the world and of persons as spiritual, then this too is still to express the matter in terms which are far too abstract. It is true that we can speak of God as the nameless and incomprehensible mystery only in very abstract terms. And for this reason too the reference of man to God, the fact that his existence is open to and orientated toward the mystery of God has of its very nature something unnameable in it. How could it be so easy to describe the path, seeing that it leads into the pathlessness of the inconceivable God? How could we find it easy to describe in words the ultimate act of man in which, surrendering himself, hoping, loving, adoring—in a word believing, he allows himself to fall into this ineffable mystery which constitutes the innermost basis, *and at the same time* the infinite remoteness of his existence that draws him out of himself? And if grace constitutes precisely that power which enabled him to achieve this making over of himself to the absolute mystery and that most special quality given by God enabling him to achieve this, how then can it be easy to speak about it in "intelligible" terms?

But one point must be emphasized about this grace precisely to the extent that it proceeds from the innermost heart and center of the world and of man: it takes place not as a special phenomenon, as one particular process *apart from* the rest of human life. Rather it is quite simply the ultimate depths and the radical dimension of all that which the spiritual creature experiences, achieves and suffers in all those areas in which it achieves its own fullness, and so in its laughter and its tears, in its taking of responsibility, in its loving, living, and dying, whenever man keeps faith with the truth, breaks through his own egoism in his relationships with his fellows, whenever he hopes against all hope, whenever he smiles and refuses to be disquieted or embittered by the folly of everyday pursuits, whenever he is able to be silent, and whenever within this silence of the heart that evil which a man has engendered against another in his heart does not develop any further into external action, but rather dies within this heart as its grave— whenever, in a word, life is lived as man would seek to live it, in such a way as to overcome his own egoism and the despair of the heart which constantly assails him. *There* grace has the force of an event, because all this of its very nature (i.e. precisely through God's grace which has all along broken open mere "nature," leading it beyond itself and into the infinitude of God) no longer has any limits or any end but (as willingly accepted) loses itself in the silent infinitude of God, is hidden in his absolute unconditionality in the future of the fullness of victory which in turn is God himself.

And precisely here one further point must be made concerning this grace which constitutes the innermost depths and the mystery of human life at its average and everyday level: this innermost dynamism of the normal "secular" life of man as it exists always and everywhere has found in Jesus of Nazareth its clearest manifestation, and in him has proved itself as real, victorious and attaining to God. And it has done this precisely in a life of this kind, in which he has become like us in all things, in other words in a life which is completely everyday in character, a life bound up with birth, toil, courage, hope, failure and death. Something which cannot be set forth *here* (though in itself it is perfectly possible to do so) is this: anyone who believes in the fact that in the human life of Jesus (and so in his death and in his resurrection as the radical dimension of *his own* everyday life) the victory of his personal life has irrevocably and definitively been promised him, and that in this (not in any other fact) the ultimate and definitive, the unsurpassable word of God has been promised him, this man also *ipso facto* (with greater or lesser degree of explicitness or implicitness) affirms in faith that which is stated about Jesus in the classic and traditional christology. A further factor *ipso facto* given in this is that anyone who seizes upon the grace of God as the radical dimension of his own personal life, as its ultimate and definitive hope, has *ipso facto* posited an assent to the historical manifestation of the definitive nature of this grace in Jesus Christ, whether or not he explicitly recognizes this definitive assent as having been posited in the dimension of his own personal history.

And finally: this grace unites us to one another in love and participation in the common lot of all. Abstracting from all more profound considerations, this is something that we recognize once we recognize that grace constitutes the innermost meaning and the holiness of the secular dimension, and this in virtue of the fact that this life, provided only that our acceptance of it is genuine, true, and loving, itself mysteriously unites us in that each one in his own personal destiny experiences and accepts that of all the rest, and conversely each one recognizes and discovers himself once he directs his gaze into the life and death of the test.

Sacrament as a Symbolic Manifestation of the Liturgy of the World

On the basis we have defined above the sacraments constitute the manifestation of the holiness and the redeemed state of the secular dimension of human life and of the world. Man does not enter a temple, a fane which encloses the holy and cuts it off from a godless and secular world which remains outside. Rather in the free breadth of a divine world he erects a landmark, a sign of the fact that this entire world belongs to God, a sign precisely of the fact that God is adored, experienced and accepted everywhere as he who, through his "grace," has himself set all things free to attain to himself, and a sign that this adoration of him takes place not in Jerusalem alone but everywhere in spirit and in truth. The sacrament constitutes a small sign, necessary, reasonable and indispensable, within the infinitude of the world as permeated by God. It is the sign which reminds *us* of this limitlessness of the presence of divine grace, and *in this sense* and in no other, precisely in *this particular* kind of anamnesis, is intended to be an event of grace. Now it is a lasting and tragic misunderstanding for us to turn these sacramental signs once more into a circumscribed enclave, such that it is in this alone that God is present, and that the event of his grace takes place.

Let us attempt to clarify what has been expressed in abstract terms by re-stating it in somewhat more concrete ones, and moreover concentrating especially upon the Eucharist. The world and its history are the terrible and sublime liturgy, breathing of death and sacrifice,[5] which God celebrates and causes to be celebrated in and through human history in its freedom, this being something which he in turn sustains in grace by his sovereign disposition. In the entire length and breadth of this immense history of birth and death, complete superficiality, folly, inadequacy and hatred (all of which "crucify") on the one hand, and silent submission, responsibility even to death in dying and in joyfulness, in attaining the heights and plumbing the depths, on the other, the true liturgy of the world is present—present in such a way that the liturgy which the Son has brought to its absolute fullness on his Cross belongs intrinsically to it, emerges from it, i.e. from the ultimate source of the grace of the world, and constitutes the supreme point of *this* liturgy from which all else draws its life, because everything else is always dependent upon the supreme point as upon its goal and at the same time sustained by it. This liturgy of the world is as it were veiled to the darkened eyes and the dulled heart of man which fails to understand its own true nature. This liturgy, therefore must, if the individual is really to share in the celebration of it in all freedom and self-commitment even to death, be interpreted, "reflected upon" in its ultimate depths in the celebration of that which we are accustomed to call liturgy in the more usual sense. This "must" primarily expresses simply that necessity in virtue of which man must accept such manifestations *when* they are present and *when* they confront him, otherwise he himself is denying and giving the lie to those existential modalities which thereby manifest themselves to his own perdition (unless he eliminates these too).

But there is a further point, just as valid and indeed still more radical: we are understanding this liturgy only in the usual sense of the term. We can only achieve a genuine enactment of it, without causing it to degenerate into an empty ritual attitudinizing, full of unbelief (so far as our participation in it is concerned) if we draw our strength from this liturgy of the world, from the liturgy of faith as expressed in concrete "this worldly" terms, which is identical with the history of the world as rightly enacted.

The Eucharistic Meal

It is in this spirit, then, that the individual goes to Mass. He is filled with the knowledge of that drama into which his life is constantly being drawn: the drama of the world, the divine tragedy and comedy. He thinks of the dying who face death with the death rattle in their throats and with glazed eyes, and he knows that even now this fate has its roots within his own being. He senses within himself the sighing of creature-hood, of the world, as it yearns for a brighter future. He entertains a feeling for the responsibility of statesmen with their decisions, which call for all their courage, and yet have to be launched into an unknown future, something of the laughter of children in their unclouded joy in the future, of the tears of hungry children, of the pains of the sick, of the disappointment of love betrayed, of the dedicated realism of scientists in their laboratories, of the dedicated austerities of those who struggle for a liberated humanity—something of all these is in him. He is also aware; even though he may be living day after day with a heart full of withered superficiality, that he *cannot* give pride of place here and now to this entire history of mankind, that even this primitive and uncultivated crudity of a dried-up heart still demands in its turn, and with anguish, to be filled with all that which moves the world. And he is not surprised when the secret essence of world history, something as it were numbing and stimulating at the same time, rises up from the depths of his own inner life and floods over the dry land of his heart. He is not surprised to find that all this too is the experience of the grace of the world, which permeates the whole of history as judgement when it is denied, as a blessed future when it is accepted, and that precisely in the Cross of Jesus it has achieved its supreme point, the point at which it is no longer possible for victory to be lost to it. In his faith the Mass attender experiences the fact that this Cross still constantly is and remains a present fact right to the end

of all history. He knows that those who mourn weep the tears
of Jesus, those in prison sit in the cell of the Lord, those who
rejoice share in the joy of Jesus, those who are lonely share
his lonely nights, and so on. He knows that it is only in this
indissoluble polarity between man and the Son of man that
mankind and he can be understood, because it is only in him
that the mystery of mankind can be grasped in its inconceivability and the hope for the future which it contains, and
because it is only in the light of the meaning of humanity and
in sharing in its lot that we can avoid degrading the presence
of Jesus in us to the level of a mere abstract ideology. The
attender at Mass, even before he has arrived at it, has already
been drawn into the drama of Golgotha that was, that is, and
that shall be, the drama that is world-wide, the drama that
has all along taken him up in its unfolding process even before
he explicitly adverts to it, that embraces "head and members"
alike, Jesus and all men in the same measure and in a relationship of mutual conditioning (albeit one that is special to
each individual). For the Son of man too is willed by God
"for our salvation" because God wills a humanity consisting
of "divine beings," because a firstborn among many brethren
is conceivable only among these many, so that the Spirit of
Jesus is from the outset the Spirit of the world as it has been
willed by God.

And so the individual goes to Mass. What is initiated there
is not something which does not exist anywhere else in the
world, but something which is there brought to manifestation
at a conscious level and celebrated in a cultic enactment,
something which really takes place in the world as God's deed
of salvation and pertains to the redeemed freedom of mankind.
The Cross of Jesus is not, properly speaking, set up afresh,
but rather its mysterious presence in the world is proclaimed.
This individual allows something which is already alive in his
heart to come to the fore, to proclaim itself. For this he
himself posits his explicit assent (even if he knows that the
most real assent—something that God and life decide and

not he through his liturgical calendar—may perhaps be posited
outside the context of cultic celebration in the compassion he
shows in his average everyday life or in those hours in which
life reaches its ultimate extremity). Under the forms of bread
and wine he offers the world in that he knows that it itself
is already ceaselessly offering itself up into the inconceivability of God in rejoicing, tears and blood. He looks with praise
at the ineffable light of God for he knows that this looking
of his only really takes place at that point at which man's
eyes see death drawing near. He knows that he is proclaiming
the death of the Lord because and in that this death, as that
which was died once and for all, is constantly present in the
world and has already been inserted into the innermost center
of the world and in a true sense continues to be died in everyone who, whether he explicitly recognizes it or not, "dies
in the Lord." He knows that in the Mass he is proclaiming
the coming of the Lord because the Lord actually *is* in the
process of coming in the world in everything which impels
the world forward toward its goal. In the holy sign he receives
the true body of the Lord in that he knows that this would
be useless if he were not in communion with *that* body of
God which is the world itself with its destiny, that he is receiving the former body so that in the reality of his own life
he may stand in an abiding communion with the latter body.
He hears and utters the word of God who reveals himself in
the Mass in the awareness that this word constitutes the
verbal expression of that word which God himself utters in
that he utters the world as his word and eternally utters
himself to this world itself in his Word. He hears this word
in the "liturgy of the word" in order that it, together with
the world, may become that other word, may utter it, hearken
to it and accept it, that word which, though it is uttered
everywhere (as nature and grace) so often falls only upon
deaf ears, and "strengthened" and in turn reflected upon in
this word, seeks to make its impact in this way too at the
human level.

A man goes to Mass. In doing so he is not necessarily called upon always or exclusively to fulfill in an explicit sense the claims of his oneness in destiny with the world and history as a whole. It can also be enough that in his conscious mind he opens himself to the depths of grace contained in that life which is his in a narrower sense. For this life too is in itself, and as part of the great drama of the world, broken into by the grace of God and orientated toward the inconceivability and absoluteness of God. In fact provided this man seizes upon this seemingly everyday life in a spirit of faith (that is in a willing and unreserved acceptance of the movement of this everyday life in itself) he experiences every day in it that this everyday life is sustained by the movement toward God. This is what takes place when someone loves unconditionally and even in situations in which his love is exploited and not returned, in which someone really forgives without "gaining anything" from it (not even the feeling of being the better man) when someone experiences the miracle of love which is bestowed upon him, he does not know why, when a man is suddenly struck with fear by some insight into the majestic inexorability of truth, when someone remains faithful to the claims of his conscience even though this faithfulness of his is exploited and used against him, and so on. In innumerable occurrences of this kind in everyday life there is always something more mysteriously present than the data yielded by direct experience. There is always a sum which defies all reckoning, an account which cannot be brought into balance by the addition of any one specific assignable item. Always in this there is a tacit reference to God who by his grace frees us in our everyday life, admitting us to his own freedom, assuming that we recognize and acknowledge this claim in our everyday life, and do so through that death which egoism can die unnoticed in our everyday lives, and assuming too that we allow ourselves to be set free for the life of God.

The individual concerned need not fear that his basic conviction of faith is under assault if he suddenly finds himself tempted to regard the sacramental rites as "empty ceremonies," if he experiences that which takes place at the altar as a "game" which, while it may be touching, initially makes the same impression upon him as the sacrificial ceremony of a Vedic priest who feeds the gods and believes that by his actions he is keeping the world in harmony with them. Faced with such temptations a Christian of this kind does not need merely to formulate an additional ideological postulate by which, so to say, he *adds on* to these rites which he seeks to keep a divine event which would not take place apart from such ritual (though in that case, surely, the divine event would not freely and personally be appropriated!). But there is something which he has to "add on in his mind," something in the light of which he must view these rites. Yet it is something which he does not have to create from his own ideology. In other words he does not, in any true sense, have to add it on in his mind at all (though he certainly can and should consciously reflect upon it). This extra "something" is the divine depths inherent in real life, which are constituted always and everywhere through the grace of God with Christ as its focal point and in the self-bestowal of God upon the world. It is from this that these rites derive, to this that they point back, and without this "something" whence they derive and toward which they tend they would truly be empty, and any other content would indeed merely be added on in the mind. He who is assailed by the fear of engaging in a ritualism which is at basis empty, which is merely filled out with ideological notions conjured up at will, must have recourse to the experience of God and of grace in his seemingly secular life, and so must say: "This experience and the "subject matter" precisely of *it* are made apprehensible at the cultic and ritual level." Obviously this presupposes that we have actually made an experience of this kind in our everyday life of the divine depths inherent precisely in this "secularity" and of the grace they bring. Anyone who says that he fails to find any such experience in his life (an experience which always comes through faith, but a faith which really is "experienced") should be answered as follows: So long as he *really* has experienced nothing of this, the sacraments must inevitably seem to him to be mere magical ritual, and according to Christian doctrine he should not even receive them, because this doctrine unequivocally forbids anyone to receive the sacraments without faith (that is without a believing experience). It would be necessary to provide such an one with instruction *and* mystagogy in the religious experience of grace in this sense, such as cannot of course be provided *in the present context*. (In this connection a point which should admittedly be taken into account is that such an individual is all along making this experience in itself, but is incapable of reflecting upon it and objectifying it in sufficient measure, and it is at *this* process of reflection and objectification that all instruction and mystagogy is aimed, and not at a process of indoctrination *ab initio*.)

The Eucharist and the Liturgy of the World

If this individual sees the Mass simply as a sign in miniature of the Mass of the world, to which obviously Christ himself belongs, then it follows that the Mass is after all not so unimportant to this individual. Only in a very conditional sense can he regard it as the "supreme moment" of his life and the source of his life. It is a "supreme moment" only to the extent that he allows God to determine *which particular* moment of his life, and under which particular "forms," whether sacred or profane, he will encounter in his life that decisive moment, that sidereal hour, in which his ultimate self-surrender to God is really achieved for him—that self-surrender which definitively determines what is to be for him for all eternity. It is a "source" only to the extent that he is aware in all this that this source is only derived from the real source of God who creates salvation in his supra-worldly and absolute primacy, and of the unique and definitive event of the death of the Lord that creates salvation. Furthermore it is a source only to the extent that in all this he knows that provided only he opens his heart in faith, hope, and love, the whole of his existence will be permeated throughout as a land from the depths of which flow the waters of eternal life. And if the objection were put to him that after all it is only at Mass that he receives the Body of the Lord really and substantially, then he would rejoin that while he gratefully acknowledges this unique gift of grace of Christ within his Church, still in responding to this substantial presence of Christ the only way in which he can avoid occupying the seat of a Judas next to the physical presence of Christ at the Last Supper is for this Lord to rise up, together with the whole yearning of the entire world and together with its destiny from the midst of his own personal life, and to bestow his grace from this (a grace that is called love for God and for mankind). This is what must take place before he can say that he is physically near to him and *also* bears witness to him in *such a way that* he loves him to the end.

But all this does not make the sacrament superfluous or meaningless. It bears witness to a truth which is otherwise so much hidden in the darkness of the world and the depths of one's conscience. It gives a better opportunity to look outward from the harmonious recollection of a cultic event into the world, and there to recognize what threatens again and again to disappear from the flagging spirit and the despondent heart within its midst. The sacrament does not dispense us from striving in the night of the world as Jacob strove by night with the angel until he had blessed him. Rather it brings home to us *the fact that* this struggle of life is a striving like Jacob's. It paves the way for, and is the promise of, the same victorious outcome. If the sacrament is the sign of the *res sacramenti*, the reality designated, which is identical with the whole unfolding history of the world (because it is a *signum commemorativum, exhibitivum* and *prognosticum*, as we may express it in the terms of Aquinas, for everything which takes place in saving history from the beginning to the end which has still to come), does it follow from this that the significance of the sacrament becomes smaller and less important than if it were a procedure of a bare individualistic pastoral care in which it was no longer possible really to believe that anything was taking place there that could really and seriously be believed in as significant for salvation? In other words could such a thing really be believed in as something which is in God's sight the definitive and irrevocable outcome of freedom, abiding and never more able to be overthrown?

Let it not be said that to celebrate the sacrament in this sense implies any denial or obscuring of its sacramental "causality." It is no denial or obscuring of the significance of the baptism of an adult either if we say that even as he enters upon it he is acting in accordance with the just claims of faith and love, and so is already justified as he comes to receive the baptism of water. Nor are we denying or obscuring the significance of the sacrament of penance when in accordance with the whole of traditional theology we say that in the normal instance the Christian approaches this sacrament of reconciliation as one who has already been justified through charity— indeed that, as Thomas Aquinas held, he must approach it in this state. Obviously Peter in no sense underestimated baptism when he conferred baptism upon Cornelius precisely *because* he had already received the Holy Spirit and not because he had not yet experienced it. In accordance with traditional theology we hold firm to the position that it is far from being necessarily the case that the recipient of the sacraments does not yet have that which the sacrament confers upon him and declares to have been conferred upon him. In this traditional formulation of the question we also really understand what is properly meant by this grace which the recipient of the sacraments already possesses, namely a state of having been drawn into the dynamic process which holds the world together, impelling it toward its goal, the inconceivability of God, uniting all earthly realities and spirits and blending them into a single history of the world as the coming of God through his self-bestowal. And it cannot be said that the approach to the sacraments suggested here in any sense tells against their significance or necessity. It may be that it is not easy or even possible to explain down to the last detail the harmony between these two truths: that of the grace which is always already present and effective from within, and that of the sacramental sign as posited from without at a particular point in time. But any theology in any case is faced with the task of showing that such a harmony exists. It is not a special difficulty arising only from the approach to the reception of the sacraments suggested here.

The Effectiveness of the Sacrament in the Sign

But in still more precise terms: What, in terms of this basic conception, is to be made of the "effectiveness" of the sacraments?[6] If we emphasize the "sign" character of the sacraments, then we are straightway in line with the best and earliest theological traditions. If we are to speak of an effectiveness belonging to the sacramental sign, then it is in accordance with this tradition that the effectiveness referred to is not to be conceived of as something added on to its "sign" function from without, but rather is to be envisaged as an effectiveness inherent in the sign precisely *as* such. The development of the modern theology of the sacraments likewise tends in this direction even in those areas in which it is in no sense concerned with the special points which are of interest to us here.[7]

This effectiveness of the sign as such (the sign of that grace of God which is already taking effect always and everywhere throughout the world right from its very roots!) can be explained in several stages. First the concrete process by which man in his physical-exteriority brings himself to his fullness in his own personal history always has from the first the character of a sign, a physical expression of that which is already present in the basic attitude of a man, *and at the same time* of the fact that there is a counter influence proceeding from the sign and affecting the basic attitude. Thus this concrete process of self-fulfilment is itself all along and in all cases a "real symbol" under which the individual brings to fruition this basic attitude of his, his *option fondamentale*. Precisely *in the fact that* he expresses himself man posits that which is expressed. In the gesture that he makes the interior disposition of the individual asserts itself. This is not simply (at least not in all cases) the *mere* subsequent promulgation such that in itself it would be unimportant for the existence of the reality promulgated. The real symbol[8] is the sign which promulgates in the unity of the body–spirit *compositum* which is man, and *at the same time* is the "cause" of that which is promulgated. It is not a cause which acts *ab externo* to posit something subsequent to and quite different from itself. Rather it is a cause to the extent that the true cause, the interior decision of freedom, can posit itself only in that it brings itself to its fullness by issuing in this its promulgation.

From this basic standpoint it is now easy to advance a step further: first all what has just been said also applies to the act of the free individual as brought to its fullness in grace. This *free individual* brings himself to his fullness as an event of grace in this sense *in that* he expresses himself, and this expression is, in the sense explained, the cause of the act imbued with grace and of the grace itself. (In the light of this the point made by the traditional established teaching of the Church is perfectly reasonable, namely that in the case of one who has already been justified receiving the sacraments, this grace—which produces a fruitful reception of the sacraments!—is always still further "increased.")

And finally: this grace is bestowed upon the world as such from its heart and center. It is constantly offered as the

innermost finality of the world's history. It unfolds itself in
the history of salvation and revelation, and brings to manifestation, and precisely in virtue of this, that which we call
the sacraments when it brings to fruition this decision, taken
in its power at decisive moments in the individual human life,
and, moreover, in a manifestation which is posited by the
Church as the basic sacrament of grace, her own nature being
fully engaged in this.[9] On this showing, then, a manifestation
of this kind is not merely a subsequent promulgation of
something which is in any case present even without such
promulgation. Rather it is something *in which* the reality
promulgated brings its own individual history to its fullness
and so extends its own real nature in that it integrates within
its own individual history more "material." In this sense,
then, the manifestation is the "cause" of that which is manifesting. Now it follows from all this that in terms of our
basic conception too a true causality, precisely a causality in
signifying (that of the "real symbol") can be ascribed to the
sacramental sign.

The Church as the Basic Sacrament of the Salvation of the World

We shall understand this whole approach still better if we
reflect upon the relationship between the world and the
Church. According to what probably is both the most relevant
and the most original statement in the ecclesiology of the
Second Vatican Council the Church is the "sacrament of
salvation" for the *world*.[10] What does this mean? The earlier
view was that the Church is the sign of salvation for those
who already positively belong to her, the sheltering ark in the
Flood of the world the sheepfold which protects the flock of
Christ and that which points the way of salvation to those
who are gathered in this ark or in this fold. On this view the

world constituted the sphere of perdition which was set over against the Church as the realm of the evil one. Now this view is certainly not regarded as simply false. There is a world which is in an evil state, a world dominated over by those principalities and powers which are hostile to God, a world made up of spirits and of men.[11] But today it is recognized more clearly that as an historical and social entity the Church is precisely not in any possible sense simply or primarily the promise of salvation for those who are "within" her. Rather she is this for those who are "still" without, and those who are perhaps destined never to belong to her in this present age in a sociological or empirical sense. For there are men who have been sanctified and redeemed by grace who have never belonged to the Church in an empirical sense, and the reason is that God never denies salvation in his grace to anyone who follows his own conscience, not even when he has not yet explicitly come to recognize the existence of God. For these men who have been sanctified and saved at an anonymous level, for these redeemed ones (there is no need whatever to use the term "anonymous Christians" if it is found unsatisfactory) the Church is the social and historical sign of salvation, the basic sacrament of that promise which applies to such as these, because she constitutes the visible community of those who acknowledge that in the deed of God salvation is victoriously present for the whole world through the death and resurrection of his Christ. Those who explicitly belong to the visible Church are not so much those who are called and predestined to salvation, as though there could not be any others similarly called and predestined. Rather they are those who, through their life, their confessing, their membership of the Church, have to make salvation manifest sacramentally to those *others* within the solidarity which embraces all men within a human race which has been redeemed by Christ. The members of the Church in the true sense work out their salvation precisely *in that* they fulfill to the full this function which they have to the rest. This does not exclude the fact that in principle all men are called to such a function, i.e. that it cannot in principle, or from the outset, be said of anyone that this particular concrete individual certainly does not enter a situation in which he develops his own individual saving history to the point at which he cannot only receive salvation, but also, precisely *in order to* receive it and to maintain it, must proclaim it too as an element in this basic sacrament called the Church.

In the light of this the relationship between world and Church is not one between the sphere of the godless and the sphere of the holy, between the Flood and the ark, but resembles rather a relationship between a hidden reality on the one hand, which is still seeking to express itself to the full in history, and on the other the full historical manifestation of this, in which that reality which, though hidden, was already present in the world achieves its own fullness in history, expresses itself, and so enters upon that mode of existence toward which it has been orientated from the outset.

The true *entelecheia* of the Church is present in the world at its innermost heart and center, but in a manner which is already recognizable to her believers in the light of her own nature. This is not to contest the fact that this hidden *entelecheia* of the Church within the world is not the "natural" dynamism of the world or of history, but rather is constituted by the grace of God—indeed ultimately by God himself in his self-bestowal upon the world. Nor is it contested that the Church is an extremely imperfect manifestation of this ultimate and victorious *entelecheia* of world history such that it is still guilty of selfishness, still precisely of such a nature that it is only gradually that it can fulfill its task of integrating within itself the particular elements in this manifestation which are constituted "outside" the Church by this grace-given *entelecheia* present within the history of the world and the history of salvation.[12]

Sacrament as Self-Fulfillment of the Church

It is on this basis that we now have to view the individual
sacraments: they are nothing else than acts in a process of
concrete self-fulfillment on the part of the Church as the basic
sacrament of salvation for the world as applicable to the
individual and to the specific situation of his own personal
life.[13] The abiding union of the Church with Christ, which
cannot be destroyed, achieves a further projection in the individual sacraments as positive concretizations of the basic
sacrament. At this level it is called *opus operatum,* which
properly speaking does not imply any opposition to the *opus
operantis,* but is rather a quality inherent in a specific *opus
operantis* (which is in fact posited both in the conferrer and
the recipient of the sacraments), the fact namely that this *opus
operantis ecclesiae* (and her minister) is posited with the
full involvement of the Church as such, and so of its very
nature cannot fall outside the sphere of Christ's grace.[14] If
therefore the sacraments are projections and actualizations
of the "sign" function of the Church as the basic sacrament,
then it follows from this that the sacraments designate and
promulgate at the level of society and history that grace which
is designated and borne witness to by the basic sacrament of
the Church. In other words they constitute signs of the grace
of the *world*, that grace which is present and effective within
the world constantly and from the first. That grace of God
which is implanted in the world also sustains the Church and
her sacraments. In the reception of the sacraments this too is
precisely something which must be "realized." If that is realized or made real, then the sacraments are no "extrinsic"
processes touching upon an unhallowed world from "without," but rather the pro-cesses (in the etymological sense!) of
the grace of the world which even within the world is perceived by him who, through word and sacrament, has experienced the fact that the life of himself and of the world has
all along been sanctified and opened up to the inconceivability
of God as no longer concealed.

The Application of the Sacrament in the Concrete Circumstances of Human Life (the Frequency of the Sacraments)

This conception, though not strictly speaking new, is intended to bring out more clearly a point which is of special importance today. Against the entire conception, however, it might be objected that it lays excessive demands upon the average recipient of the sacraments. In rejoinder it must first be said that every conception of the sacraments demands too much of the recipient. For each individual has, in the concrete circumstances of his personal life, to achieve a personal encounter with God. Yet in attempting such a thing how can he escape from having too much demanded of him on any conceivable interpretation of the sacraments? The fact that this is perhaps less clearly borne in upon us in our usual way of receiving the sacraments comes from sheer custom, which causes us to suppose that we understand and fully go through with the realities expressed by terms such as grace, means of grace, causality of the sign of grace, etc. We can freely assert that the way of approaching the sacraments put forward and recommended here demands nothing more than what is always demanded in any such approach: to realize in concrete personal terms what is meant by the grace of God, and to realize it *in such a way* that the idea of receiving such grace is also really credible. Properly speaking all that we are attempting in this interpretation is to convey a concept of grace which modern man can feel to be verifiable because it proceeds from everyday experience and regards an individualistic narrowing down of the idea of grace as something to be avoided. Of course it may be asked whether in the concrete practice of life it is possible to achieve a reception of the sacraments such as we are attempting to describe here so frequently as has been regarded as genuinely possible and worth striving for by traditional piety over many centuries (especially in the case of the Eucharist and penance). But what we are concerned with is the question of a genuine reception of the sacraments in their fullness in the concrete personal circumstances of our lives, without which any mere numerical accumulation of such receptions of the sacraments becomes meaningless. In no conceivable sense does it really increase grace, and it leads merely to a legalistic and mechanical approach to the sacramental event. But whatever interpretation we may put upon the sacrament in the concrete, this question has to be posed, and no one will find it very easy to answer. It does no harm whatever if in our devotion we avoid deciding how frequently we ought to receive the sacraments simply on the basis of the almost magical idea that the more often we receive them the better provided only that a right intention and a certain amount of good will is present, to increase the "treasury of grace" through the sacraments. Moreover, according to the way of receiving the sacraments which we are suggesting here, it is manifestly far from desirable to receive them so often as to demand too much of the recipient in the sense of over-straining his capacity to realize the significance of his act in the concrete circumstances of his personal life. But this tells against receiving the sacraments too often for us fully to realize their significance, and not against the conception we are putting forward here.[15] Each of the two factors involved must be taken as a criterion for determining the other: frequency of reception on the one hand, and genuine realization of what is involved on the other. But obviously a further factor constantly to be taken into account is the due claims of everyday life. Again the supreme point which, when it is fully achieved, can and will enable us to orientate our lives as a whole toward their final consummation is first of all exceptional and at the same time needs to be fitted into the claims of our everyday life in such a way that it acts upon us as though it were actually being achieved in the here and now. Our everyday living must very broadly approximate to that which constitutes its true significance, the supremely decisive factor in our lives, in such a way as in a certain measure creatively to anticipate such moments of radical fullness. Only in this way shall we really achieve them

aright and avoid wasting the *kairos* for them, the crucial moment at which it is possible really to receive them. The phrase
"I love you" can also be uttered in our everyday lives and
moreover should be, even though it is a phrase which properly
speaking applies to the fullness of those crucial moments in
life. And this can also be said of the sacraments, even though
when we do so we have not once more any intention of denying
what has just been said with regard to adopting a critical attitude toward an indiscrete frequency in receiving them. Presumably there are "styles" conditioned by the particular epochs
to which they belong, and determining where we strike the
balance between the supreme demand which the sacraments
in their fullness represent and so which they make upon man
on the one hand, and the tribute which the individual can
freely and willingly pay to his everyday conditions, which also
still plays its part in characterizing that which is supreme in
his own life. In fact we have no objection to make either to
the individual intercessions which we formulate in the liturgy:
on behalf of the hungry, the dying, those subjected to political
persecution, etc., even though such intercessions often seem
to come "from the heart" only to a small extent so far as we
are concerned. Should we on this account omit them, or should
we not rather allow ourselves to be warned by them ever afresh
to make sure that our hearts do not stick fast in a primitive
form of egoism (albeit perhaps a religious one)?

Religious and Secular

Now that we have put forward our theory on the basis of the
usual data of traditional theology, with all the circumstantial
details inevitably entailed in this, we should now once more
develop this theory quite simply and independently of this
our starting-point. In this way it should be possible to make
it clear far more effectively how possible it is to "realize" it
and to verify it in religious terms. Man is not in any explicit

sense endowed with religious instincts of his very nature. He easily feels all that is explicitly religious as almost impudent, and in any case excessively burdensome. Yet once we have so made clear our thesis we should be in a position to say: What is here being achieved is simply a plainer and more explicit awareness of what takes place in my life, and what precisely need not after all be suppressed or denied expression, that to which I must give my explicit adherence, however much I may be tempted to venerate all this merely silently, and however much I may be justified in claiming that there is a limit to the saving efficacy in certain forms of religious expression of this sort or in the frequency with which they are repeated. And he who is already "devout" would notice that his "spiritual life" does not constitute any dispensation from the responsibilities of his secular life, or even, properly and ultimately speaking, a point of transcendence in relation to this. Rather it is precisely the explicit taking over of this life which only seems to be secular. But it is no longer possible to set forth the conception of the sacraments we have in mind here without "taking the long way round" with the traditional form as our starting-point for the kerygmatic statement itself. This is no longer possible however desirable it may be, however true it may be that only thus would it become effective in our religious lives. In theology proper it is something else. For this always has to answer precisely for its doctrine to the earlier history of faith.

Notes

1. This special approach has to be applied within the context of a distinction which is fundamental for any sacramental theology, the distinction namely between the sacrament itself and the effectiveness of grace in personal life. To clarify this cf. also, therefore, the following articles by the author: "Personal and Sacramental Piety," *Theological Investigations* II (London and Baltimore, 1963), 109–33; "The Eucharist and Suffering," *ibid.* III (London and Baltimore, 1967), 161–70; "Formale Grundstrukturen

der Heilsvermittlung," *Handbuch der Pastoraltheologie* II/I (Freiburg im Breisgau, 1966), 55–79. Similarly E. Schillebeeckx, *De sacramentele heilseconomie* (Antwerp, 1952); *idem, Christus— Sakrament der Gottbegegnung* (Mainz, 1960).

2. The author has already discussed this question at length elsewhere. Cf. *Die vielen Messen und das eine Opfer*, Quaestiones Disputatae 31 (Freiburg im Breisgau, 2nd ed., 1966); "Messopfer und Jugendaskese," *Sendung und Gnade* (Innsbruck, 4th ed., 1966), 148–83; "The Meaning of Frequent Confession of Devotion," *Theological Investigations* III (London and Baltimore, 1967), 177–89.

3. On this cf. the author's article "Das Gebet des Einzelnen und die Liturgie der Kirche" in *Gnade als Freiheit* (Freiburg im Breisgau, 1968), 101–12.

4. On this, cf. the author's article in the present volume, "Observations on the Problem of the 'Anonymous Christian,'" and the further literature there adduced.

5. On this subject cf. chiefly the world of ideas of Teilhard de Chardin, e.g. *Hymn of the Universe* (London and Glasgow, 1965).

6. Cf. the author's article "Sakrament" V in *LTK* IX (Freiburg im Breisgau, 1964), cols. 227–30, and also in the present volume, "What Is a Sacrament?"

7. Cf. R. Schulte's summarizing article "Sacrament," *Sacramentum Mundi* V (London and New York, 1970), 378–84; also A. Winkelhofer, *Kirche in den Sakramenten* (Frankfurt, 1968). The relevant enactments, to which the Eucharist belongs, nowadays also have a decisive bearing on our understanding of the Eucharistic presence of the Lord. On this cf. the relevant studies by B. Welte, E. Schillebeeckx and J. Ratzinger. The Constitution on the Liturgy of the Second Vatican Council likewise points in this direction. Cf. the author's article "The Presence of the Lord in the Christian Community at Worship," *Theological Investigations* X (London and New York, 1973), 71–83.

8. Cf. the author's "The Theology of the Symbol," *Theological Investigations* IV (London and Baltimore, 1966), 221–52, and P. de Jong, *Die Eucharistie als Symbolwirklichkeit* (Regensburg, 1969).

9. Apart from the well-known studies by O. Semmelroth, E. Schillebeeckx and others, cf. also the author's *The Church and*

the Sacraments, Quaestiones Disputatae 9 (Edinburgh and
London, 1963), as well as "Ekklesiologische Grundlegung der
Pastoraltheologie als praktischer Theologie," *Handbuch der
Pastoraltheologie* I (Freiburg im Breisgau, 2nd ed., 1970).

10. On this, cf., among others, E. Schillebeeckx, "De ecclesia
ut sacramentum mundi," *Acta congressus internationalis de
theologia Concilii Vaticani* II, E. Dhanis, A. Schönmetzer, ed.
(Rome, 1968), 48–53.

11. Of course this "world" is also constantly present within the
sphere which we call in an empirical and social sense the Church.
This in itself should make us cautious in drawing this traditional
distinction between the realm of God and that of sin.

12. The "adaptation" of the Church to the world is at basis
the recognition of the factor of "anonymous Christianity" and of
the Church as a factor in the world and in its history, not the
condescension of the divine power stooping to a godless world.

13. The utterance of salvation is the concretization of the
basic sacrament in the life of the individual. A point constantly to
be borne in mind in this connection is that this individual, even
within the Church in which he is an element in the constitution
of the basic sacrament, always remains at once a recipient of
salvation and a seeker for salvation just as much as he who is
still "outside" it.

14. Cf. O. Semmelroth, "Opus operatum—Opus operantis,"
LTK VII (Freiburg im Breisgau, 1962), cols. 1184–86.

15. On this, see n. 2.

Johann Baptist Metz: Transcendental-Idealist or Narrative-Practical Christianity?

Theology and Christianity's Contemporary Identity Crisis

1. A Historical Crisis of Identity in Christianity? Theories, Symptoms, Reactions

There is no religion, indeed hardly any worldview, as focused on global universality as Christianity. Nevertheless, especially in these times, when human beings are becoming present more and more as *humanity*—and this not just as an idea, but in terms of real historical processes—Christianity seems to have gotten into a really serious identity crisis. Talk about a "post-religious age" or of a post-Christian world is spreading. Theories about the "sublation" of Christianity, of its disappearance, or its marginalization off into a powerless world to itself are the order of the day.

On the one hand there is the *Neo-Marxist* theory for taking on Christianity's heritage dialectically and critically, appropriating its potential for critique and liberation and its liberal-emancipatory core. In contrast to the typical and established Marxist critique of religion, for Neo-Marxism Christianity continues to be a historical force. It is even one with which we have not yet completely settled accounts; but not as a religion, but rather in its consistently secularized form as utopia, which shows itself in the liberal-revolutionary traditions.[1]

On the other hand we have the *"sublation" of the Christian religion in and through the logic of evolution (evolutionistische "Aufhebung")*. What I mean here is the theoretical reconstruction of the cultural functions (in the broadest sense) it fulfills in the history of humanity's development,[2] on the basis of that developmental logic which has been discussed at various points in this book in the interest of clarifying both its theoretical status and also its social implications.[3]

So then, around here two views on the historical fate of Christianity have been worked out. On the one hand there is the theory of the *historical discontinuity* between Christianity and the present modern age (in the interest of showing "the legitimacy of the modern age").[4] Then there is the notion of the almost unnoticeable *atrophy of religious consciousness in general*, the progressive disintegration in broad sectors of the population of religious ways of securing one's identity.[5]

It was this perspective on the situation of institutional religion (and the Christian churches in particular) that engendered the development of the theory (really the dilemma, to be precise) of the churches as "cognitive minorities":

> As far as Christianity goes, it is probably safe to say
> that the last century of Western history has brought
> with it a striking collapse in the "self-evident charac-
> ter" that Christianity once enjoyed. . . . It is not
> difficult to formulate the most important consequence
> of this in terms of a dilemma: the church, as Christian-
> ity's social "plausibility structure," can either aspire to
> adapt itself to the ways in which reality is defined in
> the world around it, or it can "wall itself off" as a
> cognitive minority. But both alternatives entail consid-
> erable difficulties given Christianity's internal struc-
> tures. The first alternative poses a decisive threat to

its spiritual content, which can only be adapted to a certain extent without completely losing its character. The second alternative is on a collision course with the self-understanding that Christianity has had, since Constantine at any rate, of being an open institution, interwoven with the whole of society in a variety of ways.[6]

These non-Christian or nontheological theories cannot be fully discussed here and rejected in a quasi-situationless and subjectless way.[7] What we do have to maintain, however, is that there are certain correspondences between these theories and the sense of crisis to be found among Christians and in the life of the church. A sense of anxiety and of doubt is on the rise, and not just among intellectuals, but among believers themselves, which is, relatively speaking, much more alarming. Is it not possible these days to observe for the first time (at least here in Central Europe), a large-scale disappearance of the kinds of faith convictions that people internalize and find deeply sustaining? Is it not now possible to find in virtually all levels of society not only the much cited "inability to mourn," but also a growing "inability to be consoled" and an inability to understand consolation as doing anything other than impotent soothing? With symptoms like these, and others as well, something of the historical identity crisis of Christianity that has been theoretically asserted appears to be showing up at the core of Christian life.[8]

The church, so it seems, is reacting more and more anxiously (at least in these latitudes). In my view the process that the church has ended up in can be characterized as "stabilizing through anxiety"—which is something that an efficient ecclesial administration can organize very easily. The danger is obvious: Stabilizing through anxiety is lacking in perspective and is moreover extremely susceptible to crises. The anonymous pressure of a situation that has gotten out of control is not being dealt with; it is only repressed.

Neither is that theological reaction of any help here that wants to interpret and evaluate this historical identity crisis in Christianity by referring to the continually contested character of Christianity, that perduring agonal situation of Christianity that every Christian has to bear in mind without any illusions. Given the concrete historical crisis, which is indeed to no small degree a crisis within Christianity itself, this observation is an abstract one. This approach can also very easily degenerate into an exculpation device, which only tries to find the causes "on the outside," and therefore does not lead to a new praxis among Christians themselves. Let us bracket here those other attempts to respond to this crisis in a direct, and in this sense "typically" apologetic way (for example neofundamentalist tendencies, which do not at all get back to a radical Christianity, but rather to a "pure" Christianity with a sectarian semantics, and so on). We will turn our view instead to what the theologically elaborated theories of contemporary Christianity are trying to do.

2. Theological Theories on Today's Christianity: A Spectrum of Positions

On the one hand there are the different forms of theological secularization theories. The modern history of "secularization" (in the broadest sense of the term) is interpreted and evaluated either as the history of Christianity's decline (this is the traditional version in Catholic theology), as a historical effect of Christianity itself, or finally even as a historical fulfillment of Christianity. Since these theological theories[9] or theses concerning secularization have already been critically discussed in chapter 2, and since (with the exception of the traditional version) they will be indirectly under discussion anyway when we look at both of the theological approaches to be taken up in a moment, let this simple listing suffice here.

The theological theories about present-day Christianity that have been worked out argumentatively and operate in a corresponding way are gathered up here under the rather ungainly cipher "transcendental-idealist." This is intended to cover approaches that are quite different and are worked out in distinct and nuanced ways: thus, the "universal history" approach and the "transcendental" approach. Perhaps I can be forgiven the "reckless" abstraction in characterizing these approaches, for the sake of clarifying, at least in outline, the concerns of a quasi postidealist, narrative-practical approach.

By the approaches that work in terms of *universal history* I do not just mean Wolfhart Pannenberg's influential (and strongly Hegelian) ontology of meaning and history, for which the "meaning of history" is not a category of practical reason, but rather (following the idealist tradition) a category of reflection.[10] To me, a conception framed in terms of idealism and universal history—in the sense of a progressively worked out history of human freedom that can be eschatologically and messianically integrated into Christianity—seems in the end also to be present in Jürgen Moltmann's impressive attempt to interpret Christianity's present situation in terms of the revolutionary history of freedom.[11] Under different premises Trutz Rentdorff's theory of Christianity, based on the liberal traditions, ultimately belongs in this category as well. Very briefly, he interprets present-day Christianity as a form in which the bourgeois history of freedom is realized and guaranteed. With all that differentiates these theories in their details, what is striking about all of them is the great care that they take to elaborate history as the locus of Christianity's identity crisis, particularly attuned, of course, to an idealist program worked out in terms of universal history.

In contrast to these, as the only Catholic theory (with an impact far outside of Catholic theology) of the present situation that has been consistently worked out theologically, there is Karl Rahner's theory of anonymous Christianity, which starts and proceeds transcendentally.[12] If it is here characterized as a *transcendental-idealist* program, and if critical questions are raised about it, then this is done in terms of the program of a practical fundamental theology that is developed in chapter 4 (among other places) as a critique of the transcendental theology of the subject. It is done in the hope that these critical questions will open up a perspective on a quasi-postidealist, narrative-practical understanding of Christianity and Christian identity. The important role that "memory" and "narrative" have in this as identity-saving categories of practical reason is discussed both in chapter 4 and in the last three chapters.

The theory of the anonymous Christian takes up the historical crisis of identity above all in the form of the dilemma posed, on the one hand, by the ever clearer social particularity of the church, and, on the other hand, by the universality of its mission and of the salvific will of God that is represented in it. Thus it seems to me that ultimately this theory is guided both by the central theological idea of an invincible universal salvific will of God's, and by the very human respect for those hidden depths of human existence which are inaccessible to absolute reflection and in which human beings remain to some extent "anonymous" even to themselves. In this theory of the anonymous Christian Rahner is really only extrapolating his transcendental conception of the person as the being drawn out of himself or herself into Godself. The human being is the being who is, so to speak, "condemned to transcendence," the one who is "always already with God" even in the acts that deny God, and whose freedom consists (only) in accepting this in faith, or suppressing it in unbelief. In the reflexive articulation of this being's freedom one absolutely has to take into account the dissonances, indeed the contradictions, between what is explicitly said and what is actually done, between freedom's act and the reflexive self-assessment or thematization of that act. We cannot delve more deeply here into this transcendental theory that Rahner developed with such profundity and rich nuances, a theory which is of course shaped by an idealist epistemology, and as a consequence can build on the traditional doctrine of *fides implicita* and *bona fides*. What we need to stick to first and foremost here is what this approach yields for Rahner in view of a theological theory of contemporary Christianity.

One must distinguish between, on the one hand, an institutionalized Christianity that grasps itself reflexively and is institutionalized in ecclesial orthodoxy, and an anonymous Christianity, on the other, in which it is absolutely the case that human beings execute a free, basic decision with regard to God, without having to grasp this decision reflexively as such, or possibly without even being able to do this. Indeed it is possible that, under the anonymous pressure of an "atheism" that is prior to the individual and to some extent structured socially, this decision might even be thematized "atheistically." For a church that even today can no longer reach many persons and that must deal with the fact that it will not make many people and groups Christian in an explicit way, this means that it can see the possibility of these persons' salvation in an anonymous Christianity of this sort.

3. Initial Questions for the Theory of the Anonymous Christian

Without contradicting what was said earlier,[13] let us now proceed immediately to some critical remarks, posed primarily in the form of questions—and only in this form, insofar as this critique is not certain that it has always attained the level of that which it criticizes, and since in any case there are not yet any alternative conceptions of equal consistency.

    1. Does not the transcendental doctrine of faith that lies at the basis of the theory of anonymous Christianity look too much like an elitist or idealist gnoseology? The "masses" of

people are saved by virtue of their *fides implicita*, by virtue of their behaving *bona fide*. The "real" context is known only by those few who have been endowed with "the exalted gift of the wise."[14] Rahner, who more than almost anyone abhorred elitism with all of his theological persona, ultimately makes this objection himself. However, his appeal to analogous "elitist" features in "the loftier perceptions in the fields of aesthetics, logic, ethics etc. [which] are in themselves truths for all, yet de facto only come to be apprehended by a minority" is not persuasive (to me).[15] Ultimately the *full* and *explicit* (!) knowledge of faith is itself a practical knowledge. In what is most distinctive to it, the knowledge of faith is incommensurable with a purely scientific and philosophical-idealist form of knowledge.[16] If one still wants to talk about an arcane knowledge when it comes to the "full" knowledge of one's faith, then this arcanum cannot be that of a philosophical gnosis. It cannot be the arcanum of an elitist idealism. Rather, it would have to be the arcanum of a practical knowledge: not the arcanum of Socrates but rather that of Jesus. To put it in a nutshell: the arcane practical knowledge of discipleship.[17]

2. In this form of "transcendental Christianity" are we not dealing with a form of over-legitimating Christianity and over-expanding its identity, in the face of the growing historical threats to its identity? Is not the historical identity of Christian faith here being bound up with a basic anthropological structure according to which the person is "always already" (*nolens volens*) with God? To be sure, it would be a fundamental misunderstanding of Rahnerian transcendental theology were one to suggest that it would introduce Christian faith only as something subsequent to an *a priori* construction of the person. As Rahner makes clear, the transcendental method goes in the opposite direction: it is the concrete historical experience in Christian faith that is universalized; it becomes the "categorial" presupposition for conceptualizing the person as the being of absolute transcendence. However,

the question remains whether a historical experience (like that of Christian faith), which by virtue of its historical character is always endangered, always threatened in its identity, can be universalized by taking a purely intellectual-speculative path, or whether this is possible only by means of a path that traverses a praxis, a praxis that cannot be theologically replaced by any transcendental reflection, but which one must, rather, "remember" and about which one must tell stories ("narrate").

In order to work out more clearly the narrative-practical Christianity toward which this points, the first thing we must do is to press this critique forward—the critique both of Rahner's transcendental-idealist theory, as well as (at least in rough outline) of the conceptions that work idealistically in terms of universal history. In so doing this critique takes particular aim at the attempt (an attempt that structures these approaches) to explain Christianity's historical identity in the final analysis in an exclusively intellectual, idealist way, without recourse to the constitutive function of Christian praxis, whose cognitive correlates are "narrative" and "memory."

4. A Fairy Tale: Read against the Grain

In order to clarify this critical intention I would like to recall one of the best-known and beloved fairy tales in these parts: the fairy tale about the hare and the hedgehog. This is the story about the bowlegged but clever hedgehog, who was walking through the field one Sunday morning. After being made fun of yet again by the hare for his bandy legs, he offhandedly suggests that they have a footrace in the furrows of the field. Then, before the race began, he runs home (for some breakfast, he said, since it is not good to run on an empty stomach), to get his wife (who, of course, looks just like him). He posted her at the far end of the field while he stationed himself at the near end, next to the hare, for the race. As everyone knows, the hare was completely taken in by the hedgehog's trick. He ran and ran in his furrow; but both at this and that end the hedgehog is "always already there." So the hare finally runs himself to death on the field.

I hope that the "little ones," the losers and the "slow ones" in life (for whose encouragement this tale was written down) will let me read this beautiful story against its own, all-too-justified intent, and let me take for just a moment the hare's side, who runs and runs, ultimately running himself to death in this footrace, while the hedgehog wins by a ruse that spares him from running at all. Making an option for the hare would be here to opt for those who are engaged in the field of history, which one covers only in the race, in the contest, in the fight (and however else the images for the historical-eschatological life of a Christian go, especially in the Pauline traditions). At the same time, this option for the hare would mean trying critically to unveil the idealist way of safeguarding Christianity's identity that ignores the identity-saving power of praxis (of running), unveiling it as a theological hedgehog trick, so to speak, which guarantees identity and victory without the experience of running (that is, without the experience of being threatened and of being undone).

5. Unveiling the Hedgehog Trick—or, a Critique of the Transcendental–Idealist Versions of Safeguarding Identity

One must distinguish two varieties of this hedgehog trick, in terms of which it is possible to explain both the transcendental attempt to get around history as well as the one that works in terms of universal history.

The *first variety* of the hedgehog trick stands for the idealist approaches that work in terms of universal history. Just as in the case of the two hedgehogs, the course of history is kept firmly in view. Since one can survey it from the perspective of both ends there really isn't any reason at all to enter into it anymore. The hare runs, and the hedgehog is sitting in a deceptive duplication at the coordinating points of the totality of history. History turns into the transparent movement of objective spirit (or of who/whatever else). And theology turns into a sort of private think-tank for world history, although, of course, one with fewer and fewer visitors and less and less public business.

Here the definitively promised meaning of salvation for history is not really disclosed "in the running." It is not invoked, remembered, and retold (for everyone) as the practical experience of history in the midst of historical life. It is frozen into a definition arrived at by reflection, which is not to be irritated by collective historical anxieties and looming catastrophes for meaning. And because of that it does not need a hope that is imbued with expectation. The present's meaning is ironed out right down to its last wrinkle, freed from all contradictions. It is "hopelessly" total, so to speak. The eschatological–apocalyptic consciousness of threat and of danger, as well as of the "misery of the age," is weak; it would appear that it was long ago successfully shifted out of the theologies of history and into the individual's history.[18]

The *second variety* of the hedgehog trick stands for the transcendental–idealist approach, for the conception of a "transcendental Christianity." The hare runs; the two hedgehogs are "always already there." In the north-German version of the fable the husband and wife take turns calling out "I'm already here" (*"Ick bün all hier"*). With their omnipresence they drive the hare to its death. Is not, however, Christianity's threatened, endangered identity here anchored and secured at a high price, at too high a price, at the price of confusing identity with . . . tautology? The two hedgehogs ("of course, the hedgehog wife looks just like her husband") stand for tautology; the running hare stands for the *possibility* of historical identity. The "running"—in which one can also get left behind—is an integral part of securing one's identity, together with the dangers it brings; it cannot be compensated for transcendentally by anything else. In my view everything else leads to tautology. The one hedgehog is just like the other; the beginning is like the end; paradise like the end of time; creation like the fulfillment. In the end the beginning recapitulates itself. History itself—with its ever threatened, vulnerable, and at any rate endangered forms of identity—barely intervenes at all. The transcendental spell is complete, and it is (like the two hedgehogs) unbeatable.[19] It thus becomes hard to avoid the suspicion that the transcendentalization of the Christian subject could be guided by a tendency to disburden and immunize that subject. Isn't the idea behind this transcendentalization to give Christianity a kind of omnipresence, an omnipresence that ultimately pulls it back from any way of being radically endangered in the field of history? Does not transcendentalizing the Christian subject take the edge off of the historical-apocalyptic struggle for Christianity and its identity? Is this struggle not prematurely eased?

6. A Plea for a Narrative–Practical Christianity

At this point, of course, one of the most decisive questions— perhaps the most decisive question—is to be presented for the first time: Can Christian theology start from anything *else* than the fact that the universal meaning of history (and therein, Christianity's historical identity) is already "firmly established"? How could the meaning of universal history still be at stake at all for theology? Is it not the case that for Christian theology history was definitively decided and saved a long time ago in the eschatological act of God in Jesus Christ? In other words, does not Christian theology *have to* talk and argue as the two approaches do that have just been criticized here—the transcendental approach or the universal history approach? Is not Christian theology in this sense necessarily idealist when it comes to history? And for the sake of its own content would it not have to prefer bearing the reproach that it does not really take history—with all its contradictions, antagonisms, its struggles and its suffering—all that seriously, that it really turns history into an "as-if-problem"? To be precise, does any other way of trying to do this not end up in the contradictory notion of a conditional salvation or to a confusion of salvation and utopia?

Because of this, people try (in these approaches as well as more generally) to treat "history" in such a way that the experience of catastrophe in history, the experience of contradictions, of nonidentity, of the possibility of collapse and failure, is shifted over to the historicity of the individual. What is at stake is only the individual's history. The individual can "apply" the eschatologically definitive history of salvation to himself or herself; he or she can also renounce it. The history of salvation subsists ahistorically, as it were. The only way it is "historical" is as an individual's history of application or refusal.

But of course, how do "solutions" of this type escape the danger of thinking of history, taken as salvation history, to some degree in terms of a subjectless totality—passing over the heads of men and women bowed down under the weight of their histories of suffering? Does not this one universal history of salvation that is grounded in Christ happen within the histories of salvation and catastrophe for subjects, within their histories as subjects? But how? And how could one talk about it were one to abstain from the image of a subjectless history when it came to the history of salvation? And finally: may the eschatologically promised deliverance of the entirety of history be whittled down in theology to a teleologically ironed-out meaning of history, in which the catastrophic elements of this history could not even be thought anymore, let alone consciously evaluated in theology?[20]

Faced with these questions I would like to make a case for the fundamental narrative-practical structure of Christianity, of its historical identity, and of the way it talks about eschatological salvation. But does not narrative have to do precisely with (individual) stories? And as a consequence, is it not the case, moreover, that stressing the narrative identification of Christian identity pushes us in the direction of individuals' stories, in which individuals apply or renounce the universal history of salvation?

This, however, is where we have to point out a crucial fact: history as a whole and the universal meaning of history can be discussed in narrative in a different way than it can in discourse alone or in argument alone. With narrative it is possible to discuss it in such a way that the talk about this universal meaning does not shift over into a drive to logical totality, into a kind of transcendental necessity, as a consequence of which the destinies of individuals, the practical histories of meaning for individual men and women, would become ineluctably secondary in comparison with a "necessary" meaning of salvation for the whole of history, and could be integrated only after the fact into the subject-less realm of this kind of definitive history of salvation. In the narrative conception of Christian salvation, history and histories, the one history of salvation and multiple histories of salvation and catastrophe, emerge together and are immanent to each other, without one truncating the other.[21] The individual histories are not devoid of a perspective on the history of salvation that has been narrated in advance; but the latter can very much take the individual histories into itself. For the narrated (and remembered) universality and definitiveness of the meaning of history does not strip the meaning from the historical praxis of resistance and render catastrophe superfluous as something that can be compensated for transcendentally or in terms of universal history. Rather, it makes that resistance indispensable.

The universality of the offer of salvation in Christianity does not have the character of a transcendental concept of universality or a concept drawn out from universal history. It has the character of an "invitation." The inviting Logos of

Christianity does not compel; it has a primarily narrative structure with a practical-liberating intention. In christological terms this means that the salvation "for everyone" that is grounded in Christ does not become universal by means of an idea, but by means of the intelligible power of a praxis: the praxis of discipleship. This intelligibility of Christianity cannot be conveyed in a purely speculative way, but narratively. Thus: narrative–practical Christianity.[22]

It may become clear at this point, to say it again,[23] that Christianity's so-called historical identity crisis is not a crisis of the contents of faith, but rather a crisis of the Christian subjects and institutions that reject the practical meaning of these contents (discipleship).

In the final analysis, this discipleship is of decisive import for that version of Christianity's identity crisis which is daily served up to it with many variations by the critique of religion and ideology critique. It is a version that been popularized (among Christians) with the slogan "Jesus, yes—church, no." What is going on here is a suspicion that has perhaps in many ways already rooted itself deeply into our pre-argumentative awareness, a suspicion that as Christianity has aged it has drifted away from its living identity with Jesus, that it sloughed off its "Christ-formedness" a long time ago, and that many of Jesus' intentions have been long ago successfully taken over by other historical movements. This suspicion cannot be alleviated simply by a better or more subtle interpretation of the way Christianity has behaved historically. No hermeneutics, however erudite, or reconstruction, however critical of its own history, will suffice. Rather, this suspicion can be alleviated only by the proof of the spirit and of power, in a consistent discipleship: that is, by a practical "Christ-formedness."[24] And the memories of Christianity's failures and the deeply rooted disillusionment over those failures—among individuals and in whole groups and classes—cannot be overcome and gotten rid of purely by explaining them. For even someone who was in the right about the historical details when it came to the memories of suffering could not by any means be counted as justified before them. This particular kind of Christian identity problem thus presses one into the praxis of discipleship and demonstrates the urgency of the concept of a narrative–practical Christianity.

At various points in this book (above all in chapters 7, 8, 11, and 12) a series of basic questions are treated that are connected to the "postidealist" version of a narrative–practical Christianity that is so briefly sketched out here. In connection with all these reflections it is also possible to give a potent rebuttal to the suspicion that what this narrative–practical way of identifying Christianity might very well come down to is a form of evasion or regression when it comes to defining historical identity. The "idealist" failure to appreciate the cognitive status of praxis as well as the practical status of narrative (and memory) as categories for rescuing identity ultimately rebounds back on the critics themselves.[25]

Notes

1. To be sure, religion is not strongly privatized here, as it is in bourgeois societies; but clearly it is radically secularized. And it is hard to see (for me, at any rate) how it could preserve its identity in this way. In the final analysis this identity is not something it has at its disposal, even from a purely historical–social perspective! Prayer and mysticism, for example, belong among the inalienable features of its identity. Whoever will no longer grant their validity and will refer to them only as nothing more than transparent forms of "false consciousness" is perpetrating a semantic deception when he or she then goes on to speak positively about religion.

2. See, for example, *Seminar: Religion und Entwicklung*, ed. C. Seyfarth and W. Sprondel (Frankfurt, 1973).

3. See chaps. 1, 4, and 10.

4. See the relevant works of Hans Blumenberg.

5. This is how Jürgen Habermas has put it in various statements in recent years, without, of course it being possible to

bring these remarks (which are sporadically present anyway)
together into a general thematization of this judgment.

6. Peter Berger, "Zur Soziologie kognitiver Minderheiten," in
Internationale Dialog Zeitschrift 2, no. 2 (1962).

7. It is not difficult to see that in its first two parts this book is
constantly confronting these theories, at least indirectly.

8. For a discussion of further symptoms of the crisis, as well as
of the reaction of the church indicated below, see J. B. Metz,
Followers of Christ (Mahwah, N.J.: Paulist Press, 1978), 29–31.

9. "Theory" is used here in that broader sense in which one
typically finds it for the self-characterization of theological
concepts.

10. For critical questions concerning Pannenberg's approach
see also the comments in chap. 4.

11. See J. Moltmann, "Die Revolution der Freiheit," in
Perspectiven der Theologie (Munich, 1968), 189–211. [This essay
is integrated, with some modifications, into a slightly longer
essay which has been translated as: "The Revolution of Freedom:
Christians and Marxists Struggle for Freedom," in Jürgen
Moltmann, *Religion, Revolution, and the Future,* trans. M.
Douglas Meeks (New York: Scribner's, 1969), 63–82.—Trans.]

12. One should consult the relevant essays in *Theological
Studies,* vols. 9–14. For a more recent discussion of this theory see
Christentum innherhalb and außerhalb der Kirche, ed. E. Klinger
(Freiburg: Herder, 1976).

13. Above all in chap. 4, section 2.

14. See the relevant formulations in Karl Rahner, "Theological
Considerations on Secularization and Atheism," *Theological
Investigations* 11, 180–82.

15. Ibid., 179.

16. On the practical structure of the idea of God see chap. 4,
section 1. What is clearly making itself felt in posing this
question is the difference in theological epistemology between
transcendental theology and a practical fundamental theology.

17. This is also the only way of avoiding the danger of turning
the full knowledge of faith (viz., "orthodoxy") into an orthodoxy
of elites, which could never become an actual orthodoxy for the
people. It could be at best a care-giving orthodoxy of a feudal
church "for the people," but never an orthodoxy for a "church of

the people," in which the people is itself the adult subject of its own religious identity (see chap. 8).

18. See here the theses in chap. 10.

19. Of course I do not think that Karl Rahner's theology is tautologically deceptive—any more than, say, Karl Barth's. See the excursus to chap. 12.

20. The all-too-carefree dealings with the category of "meaning" (especially "the meaning of history") in theology have to be critically interrogated. Indeed, "meaning" has come to be theologians' favorite child, and now, like all favorite children, it is all too readily coddled and overestimated. If one concedes that not even theology can do without this category, it must never be forgotten that it cannot thereby be a matter of an unendangered meaning, which one could pull out of one's ironclad treasure vault, say of ontology, whenever one wanted, when it really ought to be introduced and "described" by the intelligible power of Christian action itself. There is a way of securing meaning that is neither transcendental nor works in terms of universal history! The theological treatment of the question of meaning must not mislead us into a quasi objectification of "meaning," into simply ignoring the problem of rescuing meaning or ignoring the historical threats to the reserves of meaning, and forgetting— through a lack of apocalyptic consciousness—that the one toward whom the Christian expectation of meaning is directed does not just return as the one who fulfills the Kingdom of God, but also as the one who overcomes Antichrist. This would mean that Christians in particular would have to be mindful of something that Ernst Bloch urged on us by inverting a well-known phrase of Hölderlin's: "Wherever the salvific approaches, danger grows as well."

21. This "narrative mediation" also seems to me to be of great significance for a Christian theology of religions. To be specific, narrative–practical Christianity can hold on to its eschatological–universal history of meaning in encountering these other religions, without thereby having to monopolize the histories of these other religions in terms of a "totality of meaning."

22. For a more detailed discussions of the fundamental narrative–practical structure of Christology see Metz, *Followers of Christ*, 39–44.

23. See chap. 4, section 1.

24. [Metz alludes here to Gotthold Ephraim Lessing's famous essay "On the Proof of the Spirit and of Power," *Lessing's Theological Writings*, ed. and trans. Henry Chadwick (Stanford: Stanford University Press, 1956), chap. 5, n. 3.—Trans.]

25. See chap. 4, section 2.

III

Theological Grounding
for a Spirituality of Life
Engaged with the World

Karl Rahner's theological project can be read in part as a response to the anti-religious dimension of the Enlightenment, the conviction that religion is alienating and that religious authority suppresses human autonomy. To this, Rahner's theology offers a retort: The closer human existence is to God, the more fully human it becomes, because God is precisely the creator and the promoter of human freedom and autonomy. Rahner's theology of grace argues for God's personal presence and positive impact on human beings, urging creativity and historical development. God as Spirit acts as the sustaining ground of the world's evolution. Jesus Christ represents and mediates this presence of God to human consciousness so that, even within the negative dimensions of human existence, including death itself, the presence of God abides, and with it the power of the promise of resurrection.

The first level for appreciating the theology and spirituality of Rahner should be an appreciation of the grandeur of this vision of reality and how, concretely, it can support each person's life. The notions of grace, the unity of love of God and love of neighbor, and the dynamics of formal sacrament, worship, and religious practice are all situated within the framework of the relation between God and the world developed in his theology of grace. Rahner's spirituality digs down into a theological anthropology that views the human as suffused with the personal presence of divine love. Grace symbolizes the presence and work of God in the world, not as an intermittent agent but as gracious divine Spirit in an embracive accompaniment and dialogue with the world. The guidelines for an active Christian spirituality of engagement with the world flow from Rahner's large vision of God as Spirit and grace encompassing the world in love.

Somewhat analogously to Dorothee Soelle's relationship with Rudolf Bultmann's existential interpretation of the Bible,[1] Johann Baptist Metz relates to Rahner's theology in a way that both presupposes him and opens his thinking into a wider social framework of mutual interdependence in historical existence. These two theologians, Rahner and Metz, as represented in these texts, do not have to be understood as in competition with each other. They open each other's thinking to deeper understanding and more extensive relevance. The interpretation of that relevance which follows calls attention to a number of basic insights which highlight how a social-existential (Metz–Rahner) and a personal-political (Rahner–Metz) theology can open up the possibility of a deep experience of being related to God in the very course of exercising one's freedom, creativity, and social engagement with the world.

The theme governing this interpretation of how Rahner's and Metz's theologies bear significance for spirituality today is expressed in the title referring to theological grounding for a spirituality of life engaged with the world. Both of these theologians could claim this as the aim of their theologies. But this open topic can be narrowed. The accent falls on lifting up aspects of their thought that underline the potential of spiritual value in public, professional, and personal action in the world.

God Is within the Secular

The meaning of *secular* has to do with time, the temporal order of things, which more and more is considered autonomous.[2] Analogous to a separation of church and state, the practical spheres of everyday life possess an internal logic that does not brook interference from the outside. In Christianity's theology of creation, God authorizes the autonomy or value-in-itself of creatures and becomes the guardian of their identity. That appears readily in the valuation of individual persons, but it also carries over into eco-theology. It requires some acuity to appreciate how the relationship to the God of creation in one sense denies the autonomy of created being and in another sense protects the autonomy of everything that exists from the illegitimate encroachment of other creatures. This is especially delicate in Darwin's description of the mechanics of evolutionary life. But some transcendent arbiter is required to prevent a reduction of human life to the big swallowing the small. This delicate relationship offers an insight into the very nature of human spirituality.

The doctrines of creation and salvation express this tensive conviction, but Rahner consistently appeals to the theology of grace to make this point. Grace is not merely God's presence but God's personal presence or communication of God's self. The nearest analogy here is intersubjective communication across physical or bodily media, when one freely, without dissimilation, opens oneself to another. This, of course, cannot be imagined concretely because of God's transcendence. But this analogy opens up a principle of life-changing import: One can find God mixed up in the most secular of situations. Spirituality begins by reflectively entering into the activities of human life and recognizing that in dealing with them one is also negotiating one's identity in the presence of God. Love of neighbor *is* love of God. The principle applies to both positive and negative experiences: reaction to birth and death; good health and energy on one side and sickness and weakness on the other; failure and success in creativity and achievement; sin when it is recognized as sin; and the most serious temptations to despair in contrast to those high points that invite gratitude. God is present in all of it.

Rahner's faith, then, is faith in humanity, despite everything, because of the God revealed in Jesus and the tradition that formed Jesus. This radical and ultimately hopeful commitment to the human flows from the groundwork of Rahner's Christian spirituality, and Metz shared it.

God Is within Freedom[3]

A crucial element of the discussion of religion and spirituality in the modern era is freedom. Enlightenment writers often saw religion as authoritarian curtailment of human creativity. Freedom became the mantra of modernity. In Rahner's thinking, one encounters God most deeply within human freedom and its exercise. The previous reflection focused on objective situations in which one could encounter God. But the base of Rahner's reflection is "transcendental"—that is, he appeals to what seem to be universal structures of human experience. Despite Rahner's intellectualism, his deep reflections on the metaphysics of knowledge orient it toward freedom and committed practice. Freedom, for Rahner, cannot be reduced to choice. It refers to the open space of the human spirit's presence to itself, where it discovers power for its creativity and responsibility for its agency.

In Rahner's theology of grace or God's communication of God's self to each person, the presence of God manifests itself through reflection on the opening up of freedom to self-transcending action in the world. Rahner's view of grace retrieves Augustine's "cooperative grace" and Bernard of Clairvaux's view of grace as the internally supporting agency of God within freedom. God is not a competing agent in the world but the transcendent impetus for what the modern secular world cherishes most deeply: human acting, doing, creating, and achieving. Rahner retains the teleological and activist spirituality of Aquinas: We are created to move toward our destiny through our actions. But he emphasizes how the whole of the human enterprise is supported by and riding upon the inner power of God's presence. Ironically, God's power renders what human beings do valuable, important in themselves, which they ultimately cannot be without God. Metz did not abandon these convictions.

The Spiritual over the Religious

Rahner's fundamental vision or viewpoint rearranges Christian life. This is carefully argued in both of his texts: God is encountered in relationships with others, and this relationship with God is brought to the assembly for worship. Despite appearances, one does not "first" encounter God in church but in the world. In terms of Bonhoeffer's "world come of age" and the popular American cliché "spiritual but not religious," *spirituality* refers to the way persons and groups live their lives in relation to what they deem ultimate. Rahner's formula transfers the operative core of Christian life in our secular world from a "religious" life to a "spiritual" life. In this new framework, religiosity, in the sense of organized practice, emerges out of spirituality and possesses authentic value only in the way it relates back to spirituality. Formal religious practice is not where one primarily encounters or responds most deeply to God. The point does not discount the experiential power that public worship can generate. It refers, rather, to what the gospels repeat over and over again: that actualized union with God occurs within secular life itself, particularly in moral response to the neighbor. This completely revalues secular life. It also puts formal religious life in its proper perspective, as gathering, remembering, and reflecting on a spiritual life sustained and promoted by God in the world. Luther's spirituality of gratitude fits neatly into this description of assembly and worship.

Factoring a Social Anthropology into Spirituality

Enter Metz.[4] Rahner and Metz are far from identical, but they are plants springing from the same soil at different times addressing different cultural issues. We need a metaphor to symbolize the expansion of meaning when some of Rahner's ideas are transposed from an experienced personal anthropology to a public, social matrix wherein a new set of assumptions and dilemmas face the questioner. Something more radical than a shift of key in a musical composition occurs in this transposition, and something deeper than a new emphasis in an old argument. What Metz brings to Rahnerian spirituality springs from new exigencies that Metz communicated in the story of his military experience. Like Dorothee Soelle, Metz is dealing with the Holocaust. What had happened in Christian Europe?

Other issues lay beneath a changed Europe. Cultures became more pluralistic, and the mix of religious diversity within a shared society weakened public support for any given religious faith and forced it into a closer internal sphere supported by smaller groups. Faith required more internal fortitude and personal responsibility in order to coexist with other different faiths in a secular world. Metz rejected a privatization that can accompany secularization, reduce the spiritual to one's private thoughts, and remove public issues from the sphere of faith's concern. Metz attacked the explicit withdrawal of transcendent spiritual value from the public, secular, and common weal. This separates the spiritual relevance of one's deepest faith from most of human preoccupation.

The point here does not lie in depicting Rahner's theology as individualistic; this would be a confusion about the character of transcendental thinking. What Metz brings to the fore consists of a recognition that the social sphere is not an add-on to a personalist synthesis. Human experience itself is social.[5] A good example of this is the language that structures each person's thought. The social dimension of experience means that all facets of human life, most importantly the social relationships that bind human beings together, are involved in the most basic of human responses. Before the question of how to make the values of Christian faith operative in a shared and pluralistic human society can be addressed, it has to be established that a Christian spirituality that neglects these dimensions in that measure falls short of what it should be. Christian faith and its symbols have a bearing on the social, cultural, and political spheres that determine so many basic patterns of human life. Those relationships, which socially transcend each individual, have to be factored into moral and spiritual thinking in order to correspond with reality. In short, spirituality itself is social and has to be responsive to social problems in order to be relevant to the world in which people actually live.

In a concise formula, Metz expressed how, in a reflective moment, one may become aware of the negative structures that are part of a particular culture. "The essential dynamism of history is the [1] memory of suffering as a negative awareness of [2] the freedom that is to come, and [3] as a stimulus to act within the horizon of this history in such a way as to overcome suffering."[6] This is a description of moral perception; it is so broad that one can see it at work in some measure in all ethical discernment. The pervasiveness of this moral logic shows that a failure to enter into this sphere of discernment effectively curtails the relevance of faith itself to human spirituality. More positively, one may look at Metz's formula as describing three dimensions of an integrated Christian spirituality that responds well to the present situation and to Bonhoeffer's question of what a Christian spirituality has to look like in the present world come of age. The three stages are recognition of the affront of human suffering, imagining a better future for human freedom, and contributing to achieving it. They are reflected in what follows.

A Prophetic Spirituality of Interruption

The popular view of religion in developed secular cultures depicts it as a private matter and, unless well organized, largely irrelevant to society as such. It can also be a conservative force in society that only acts up when its public moral norms are contradicted. It can also be a liberal force in society in defense of members of its constituency. Intrinsically, Christian faith contains a potential and frequently an actual dimension of subversion of the status quo. Faith in God demythologizes idols, everything that poses as a this-worldly absolute. Faith in the God of the Bible summons the prophetic dimension of criticism. Human suffering jolts this dimension into action. God stands for life against all the forces of death and human diminishment in history. God's will does not correspond to the ways of society when they institutionalize prejudice; God can motivate radical reaction. What Metz calls a *dangerous memory* of innocent suffering awakens conscience, interrupts the status quo, and prompts a quest for justice.

Positive Spirituality Inspired by Jesus's Ministry

The logic of a negative experience is such that it implicitly presupposes that one knows something is wrong by contrast with what could be or should be. But people can agree that something is wrong in the present situation without having any clear idea of what should replace it or where a positive alternative might lie. The creativity of imagination and reason provides endless possibilities for viable resolutions. The faith traditions appeal to their positive foundations and histories for values that inform moral discernment. In theistic traditions, the appeal is to God's will, but each tradition has a distinct perspective on what that might be.

The Christian turns to the ministry of Jesus of Nazareth for a set of ideals that enable a discernment of God's values. Here Jesus stands in the Jewish line of God's prophets. He does not simply represent God's wisdom in the sense of the intelligibility of the status quo. He is also the voice of God's judgment. The God that Jesus represented is not a God who set up an established order and seeks to preserve it. He portrayed a God who stands for critical awareness within the community of all of God's own people. Those who benefit from a social order tend to deny connection with those on the margins. People who are relatively secure and financially stable tend to view God as the creator of the order of the universe and the guardian of the well-being they possess. Against this Metz maintains that, in a community of human solidarity and interdependence, one cannot simply abdicate concern for suffering members and assign it to others, especially when it is systemic.

Jesus's message is clear: Innocent suffering for which human beings are responsible either actively or passively is wrong. Jesus represents God's perspective on human dignity and turns it into a commandment for change. Jesus presents God as the ground for motivating people to do new things and to alter the future. The radical side of Jesus, his critique, tends to be blurred by time, but this impulse in the Christian tradition comes from him. It is not read into the gospels but appears in his attention to the poor and marginalized and his appraisal of insensitive leaders. In the face of human suffering, Jesus turns God around and represents God's moral challenge to all who are content and unconcerned about others. In situations of systemic social suffering, interpreting the God of everyday life has to read God's will or rule as demanding changes that fundamentally reorient consciousness, motivation, and behavior.

A Spirituality of Action: Exercising Freedom

The theme of a reciprocity between contemplation and action has accompanied Christian spirituality from the beginning; it is part of the Jewish tradition and a tension of life itself. But it has been transformed in contemporary culture. Life in the developed world consists of uninterrupted activity. There is no time for contemplation; one "makes time" for Sunday worship and tries to fit it in. The balanced alternation between contemplation and action, or even the idea of contemplation in action, seems like a dream from an underdeveloped agricultural world. It neatly described the rural monastic life. Is a spirituality that is deep or really mindful of transcendence compatible with the pragmatic hyperactivity of contemporary culture?

One way of adjusting the conception of Christian spirituality to actual life consists of correlating the language with social and cultural possibility. The slogans of the past said that faith should be followed by or converted into action; by their fruits you shall know them; not what people say but what they do; we must transform passive faith into a faith that performs. If people are constantly exhausted and too preoccupied even to know where their real faith lies, it may be better not to presuppose that ordinary Christians possess what has been a traditional kind of faith. What would it mean to recognize that one's activity actually contains a person's actual faith, and to ask about the content of the faith that one actually lives by?

Finding an answer to these questions may require a new starting point rather than trying to fit contemporary behavior into old formulas. The number of people today who have a clear set of Christian beliefs that guide their lives may be overestimated. A person's actual spirituality *is* the way they live their lives. The spirituality is the human action. In our pluralistic societies, belief systems are relativized, and spiritual creativity may be a better description of what is really going on. Instead of asking whether spirituality corresponds with set beliefs, one might better examine the implied beliefs that are contained in an actual spirituality. Human identity lies embedded in activity; so does one's actual relationship with God insofar as it is within human control. Human activity is less putting into practice something that already exists and more intentional commitment and action that constitutes the distinctive value and identity of the self and one's response to God. A narrative theology suggests that the analysis of actual spirituality, whether personal or social, begins with an analysis of actual behavior rather than with the ideals of what it should be.

In sum, Metz proposes a narrative theology, which translates into theology grounded in a spirituality of action, anchored in the values to which persons actually commit and dedicate their lives, and responsive to one's membership in society. Traditionally, ministers of the gospel urged people to convert their faith into action. One can hardly argue against that. But it may make more sense to Christians in a culture of frenzied activity to hold the mirror of Jesus's values and activity to the values for which people invest so much of their energy today. If activity defines identity, the quality of the activity defines the character and deeper identity beneath the persona and group with which one identifies.

God and the Activity of Social Engagement

The point of political theology does not lie in activity per se, but in how activity motivated by Christian faith relates to the many social structures that suffocate life in the people they are meant to serve. It is one thing to say that the theology and spirituality of social engagement supply the motivation for those few people who are social activists, who chose as their life's work to be leaders and catalysts for social change in favor of the poor and so many other marginalized groups. But how does the gospel of social engagement have general application: Does it transcend a subset of Christian activists? How does social engagement reach across social stratification and into the enormous variety of jobs and cultural lifestyles to resonate in some meaningful way with everyone? If the social imperative of the gospel is intended for all, how can a Christian spirituality that demands social action on the part of all followers of Jesus be internalized across the spectrum of persons who are all unique and occupy such diverse places in society? The answers to these questions can be divided into two parts: The first is personal and responds in terms of each person's internalizing a social consciousness in his or her unique way; the second is social and relates to corporate feasibility.

The immediate purpose of a narrative theology is to understand Christianity in a way that generates or stimulates an active, engaged Christian life of service in society. The first obligation of a theology of the spiritual life consists of explaining Christian faith in a way that intrinsically entails concern for the victims of social discrimination and bias. This concern describes an aspect of both the content of Christian revelation and faith and its subjective appropriation in people's lives. Few theologians have made the point of the social relevance of faith in God more strongly than Karl Rahner in his statement of the identity of love of God and love of neighbor. Metz preserves that argument and explicitly extends it into the social-existential context that defines each person. One cannot coherently love one's neighbors and be content with the policies that cause their suffering. In a deeply individualist culture, people can and do ignore the social dimensions of moral sensibility. They also propose social solutions from partisan perspectives. But nothing excuses the absence of a social dimension of spirituality in the churches or in their pulpits. This is more easily said than actually corrected; churches are always to some degree prisoners of their cultures. But it helps to be clear about principles. Social concern is intrinsic to the gospel, and every Christian should be exposed to Jesus's teaching and feel the responsibility for appropriating it.

The second obligation has to be realistic and wise in the exercise of a prophetic imagination.[7] Both the theologian and the preacher have to take the measure of their audience, both in terms of the people they are addressing and the society in which they exist. Many major urban centers of the world today are religiously pluralistic or not religious at all; and a feasible social-ethical dimension of the gospel, if it is not sectarian, has to find a common language. On the one hand, the public face of Christian social commitment has to be rooted in God, but its presentation cannot be partisan if it is for the common good. The stimulus for Christian engagement appeals to the values of the rule of God that Jesus taught. The theologies of Rahner and Metz show how actual social action is spiritual when it transcends blind activism and is guided by careful ethical reflection.

On the other hand, Christian spirituality has to be committed to justice for all constituents in society, without being reduced to a social-service organization. By definition, situations of social injustice mean that some group or segment of society is not being served by the social systems or is actually harming them. Behind a socially ethical impetus to action and an integrally humane spirituality lies an image of God portrayed in Jesus's ministry. The gospels are full of stories of Jesus representing the segments of society that do not participate in the common good and are socially marginalized. Christian spirituality must take the side of the victims of social injustice, even when the ways of doing so in an effective way may not be immediately apparent. The church is not a society for ethics and culture but a tradition of Christian faith in God, who is the ground for ethical commitment and the promotion of a culture of justice. The church cannot be partisan in the sense of identifying with a specific political party lest it lose its critical edge and fail when the party fails.

Resurrection Hope

A theological reflection on the role of time, history, and the future in the spiritualities of Rahner and Metz will supply grounds for hope. Rahner's theology places the fundamental moral disposition of hope at the center of his anthropology. Hope lies grounded in the openness of the human subject to existence itself. Since existence is subject to time, always moving out of the past and into the future, each person and the species as a whole are in motion and intrinsically temporal. Hope essentially consists of positive acceptance of one's actual condition. The idea of a stable monolithic world or humanity is dead; everything is always in motion; time is a constituent of being rather than a container. This newly discovered parameter for understanding reality has provided an equally new framework for a retrieval of Aquinas's teleology: We are all moving forward in time toward our destiny.[8] The intrinsic character of temporal movement bestows new importance upon an eschatological and an apocalyptic imagination wherein God is not only transcendent Presence but also, from our perspective, "up ahead" as the absolute finisher of existence. The projection of what we should be and hope to become fuels dissatisfaction with our greatest failures but also stimulates creativity and positive construction.

Christian faith finds in its tradition a model for its hope in the future in Jesus's resurrection. *Resurrection* means the reawakening and preservation of what went before. Resurrection thus affirms in the most radical terms available that human life is valuable, that human work has eternal value, that human spirituality as what we do is ultimately important. This real but transcendent rather than empirical event that is recognized as Jesus's destiny is a definitive testimony to God's promise of ultimate salvation that had been constantly announced in the Jewish prophets and is understood by many today to include all people. Christianity consists in the collective hope for an absolute future as symbolized in the resurrection of the crucified one: *memoria passionis et resurrectionis Jesu.* The Latin phrase thus symbolizes both a spirituality and a comprehensive theology of history.

But does not an absolute confidence in resurrection deliver an element of contentment because everything will be all right in the end? Does not resurrection cover over the actual history that should disturb us? Ashley puts the question to Metz:

> [S]hould not God's decisive salvific action in and through Jesus give some kind of certainty about the outcome of history? Yes, but for Metz it is a certainty that takes the form of a resolute *hope* for the future that is tested and proven by acting in history as disciples, rather than the knowledge of the fact about history's outcome that one could entertain from outside the fray. It is *narrative*, Metz claims, that is most able to present this confidence and hope in the ultimate victory of God in history, without ironing out the dangers and risks that . . . give the narrative its drama, its verisimilitude and credibility, its meaningfulness.[9]

To sum up, the texts illustrating the theological grounds of Christian spirituality in Rahner and Metz do not collapse either one into the other. In fact, the differences between Metz and Rahner widened as Metz continued his work. But these selected texts show how the impact of massive social dehumanization draws Christian spirituality out of any kind of a private zone and forces reaction to the actual dynamics of history. The common ground beneath the texts offers an interpretation of a theological foundation for a Christian spirituality that engages history.

Notes

1. Dorothee Soelle, *Political Theology* (Philadelphia: Fortress Press, 1974).

2. It is almost irresponsible to use the term *secular* as if it had a stable meaning. Secularity and secularization can be approached through several different disciplines, and they are controversial within most of them. The term *secular* is used here to refer to what pertains to the practical temporal order of things, often in contrast to religious or spiritual affairs. But the intent here is to overcome or at least soften that antithesis and/or to see it in a positive light.

3. Like the term *secular*, *freedom* should be narrowed down more than it can be here. In this discussion it refers to what appears in the self-reflective character of the human, the ability to so objectify the self in consciousness that we can conceive of our own autonomous agency relative to the world.

4. He was far from the first to enter. Walter Rauschenbusch did something analogous in his evangelical and socialist way; before him was Anglican social Christianity in the nineteenth century; a tradition of social Christian thinking goes back to Jesus addressing Israel, and before him the prophets. The point here relates to the joint witness of Rahner and Metz and how transcendental and narrative spiritualities can be merged independently of Rahner and Metz.

5. This does not imply that Rahner was hostile to these ideas; they are entailed in the proposition that love of neighbor is love of God when, as Jesus taught, even our enemy is our neighbor.

6. Johann Baptist Metz, *Faith in History and Society: Toward a Practical Fundamental Theology* (New York: Crossroad Publishing, 2007), 104. In context, Metz proposes this three-dimensional logic as a dynamic of social history. But it also reflects a process of a personal coming to awareness of an evil situation, when compared with what should be, and a desire to participate in overcoming the suffering. The logic actually describes common experiences whether they be social or interpersonal.

7. Not necessarily prudent; there is no such thing as a prudent prophet. The point is effectiveness; wisdom and realism are aimed at results.

8. The idea of teleology becomes somewhat ambiguous in the world described as evolutionary and in a historically conscious anthropology. Teleology can no longer be based simply—that is, without further discussion, on the analogy of a single designer of a prescribed goal. But this is not the place for such a complex discussion.

9. J. Matthew Ashley, in Metz, *Faith in History and Society*, 236–37.

Further Reading

Ashley, J. Matthew, "Johann Baptist Metz," in *The Wiley Blackwell Companion to Political Theology, 2nd ed.* Ed. William T. Cavanaugh and Peter Manley Scott. Hoboken, NJ: John Wiley & Sons, 2019 (online, 2020): 236–49. [Ashley describes Metz as a practical fundamental theologian who writes against the background of theodicy to show that to resist suffering and find meaning demands a framework of hope in an absolute future.]

Downey, John K., Steve T. Ostovich, and Johann M. Vento, eds. *Facing the World: Political Theology and Mercy.* New York: Paulist Press, 2018. [Written in honor of Metz, this collection of essays turns to the themes of incarnation, interruption, recognition and mercy as a basis for a spirituality in our time.]

Dych, William V. *Karl Rahner.* Collegeville, MN: Liturgical Press, 1992; London: Continuum, 2000 (online). [A guide to the life and thought of Rahner by the English speaker who best knew his thought and was able to make it accessible to a wide audience.]

Marmion, Declan, and Mary E. Hines, eds. *The Cambridge Companion to Karl Rahner.* New York: Cambridge University Press, 2005 (online, 2006). [This resource offers interpretations of Rahner on standard theological topics; of special note are the theological grounds of spirituality and the experience of grace.]

Metz, Johann Baptist, "Theology in the New Paradigm: Political Theology," in *Paradigm Change in Theology: A Symposium for the Future*, ed. by Hans Küng and David Tracy. Edinburgh: T&T Clark, 1989. [Metz speaks for himself in describing the dynamics of his political theology.]

Metz, Johann B. *A Passion for God: The Mystical-Political Dimension of Christianity.* Ed by J. Matthew Ashley. New York: Paulist Press, 1998. [This collection of self-defining essays by Metz explains the spiritual impetus behind his theology of engagement with the world.]

O'Meara, Thomas F. *God in the World: A Guide to Karl Rahner's Theology.* Collegeville, MN: Liturgical Press, 2007. [This book by an eminent theologian shows why Rahner's theology of a God immanent within the world is as relevant today as when he wrote in the mid–twentieth century.]

Rahner, Karl. *Encounters with Silence.* Westminster, MD: Newman Press, 1960. [This relatively early work in spirituality is often suggested as a first introduction to his intellectual construction.]

Schuster, Ekkehard, and Reinhold Boschert-Kimming, eds. *Hope against Hope: Johann Baptist Metz and Elie Wiesel Speak Out on the Holocaust.* New York: Paulist Press, 1999. [This short book, which puts Metz in conversation with Elie Wiesel, opens up the foundations of Metz's spirituality in hope in the face of tragedy and suffering.]

About the Series

The volumes of this series provide readers direct access to important voices in the history of the faith. Each of the writings has been selected, first, for its value as a historical document that captures the cultural and theological expression of a figure's encounter with God. Second, as "classics," the primary materials witness to the "transcendent" in a way that has proved potent for the formation of Christian life and meaning beyond the particularities of the setting of its authorship.

Recent renewed interest in mysticism and spirituality have encouraged new movements, contributed to a growing body of therapeutic-moral literature, and inspired the recovery of ancient practices from Church tradition. However, the meaning of the notoriously slippery term "spirituality" remains contested. The many authors who write on the topic have different frameworks of reference, divergent criteria of evaluation, and competing senses of the principal sources or witnesses. This situation makes it important to state the operative definition used in this series. *Spirituality is the way people live in relation to what they consider to be ultimate.* So defined, spirituality is a universal phenomenon: everyone has one, whether they can fully articulate it or not. Spirituality emphasizes lived experience and concrete expression of one's principles, attitudes, and convictions, whether rooted in a defined tradition or not. It includes not only interiority and devotional practices but also the real outworkings of people's ideas and values. Students of spirituality examine the way that a person or group conceives of a meaningful existence through the practices that orient them toward their horizon of deepest meaning. What animates their life? What motivates their truest desires? What sustains them and instructs them? What provides for them a vision of the good life? How do they define and pursue truth? And how do they imagine and work to realize their shared vision of a good society?

The "classic" texts and authors presented in these volumes, though they represent the diversity of Christian traditions, define their ultimate value in God through Christ by the Spirit. They share a conviction that the Divine has revealed God's self in history through Jesus Christ. God's self-communication, in turn, invites a response through faith to participate in an intentional life of self-transcendence and to co-labor with the Spirit in manifesting the reign of God. Thus, *Christian spirituality refers to the way that individuals or social entities live out their encounter with God in Jesus Christ by a life in the Spirit.*

Christian spirituality necessarily involves a hermeneutical task. Followers of Christ set about the work of integrating knowledge and determining meaning through an interpretative process that refracts through different lenses: the life of Jesus, the witness of the scripture, the norms of the faith community, the traditions and social structures of one's heritage, the questions of direct experience, the criteria of the academy and other institutions that mediate truthfulness and viability, and personal conscience. These seemingly competing authorities can leave contemporary students of theology with more quandaries than clarity. Thus, this series has anticipated this challenge with an intentional structure that will guide students through their encounter with classic texts. Rather than providing commentary on the writings themselves, this series invites the audience to engage the texts with an informed sense of the context of their authorship and a dialog with the text that begins a conversation about how to make the text meaningful for theology, spirituality, and ethics in the present.

Most of the readers of these texts will be familiar with critical historical methods which enable an understanding of scripture in the context within which it was written. However, many people read scripture according to the common sense understanding of their ordinary language. This almost inevitably leads to some degree of misinterpretation. The Bible's content lies embedded in its cultural context, which is foreign to the experience of contemporary believers. Critical historical study enables a reader to get closer to an authentic past meaning by explicitly attending to the historical period, the situation of the author, and other particularities of the composition of the text. For example, one would miss the point of the story of the "Good Samaritan" if one did not recognize that the first-century Palestinian conflict between Jews and Samaritans makes the hero of the Jewish parable an enemy and an unlikely model of virtue! Something deeper than a simple offer of neighborly love is going on in this text.

However, the more exacting the critical historical method becomes, the greater it increases the distance between the text and the present-day reader. Thus, a second obstacle to interpreting classics for contemporary theology, ethics, and spirituality lies in a bias that texts embedded in a world so different from today cannot carry an inner authority for present life. How can we find something both true and relevant for faith today in a witness that a critical historical method determines to be in some measure alien? The basic problem has two dimensions: how do we appreciate the past witnesses of our tradition on their own terms, and, once we have, how can we learn from something so dissimilar?

Most Christians have some experience navigating this dilemma through biblical interpretation. Through Church membership, Christians have gained familiarity with scriptural language, and preaching consistently applies its content to daily life. But beyond the Bible, a long history of cultural understanding, linguistic innovation, doctrinal negotiations, and shifting patterns of practices has added layer upon layer of meaning to Christian spirituality. Veiled in unfamiliar grammar, images, and politics, these texts may appear as cultural artifacts suitable only for scholarly treatments. How can a modern student of theology understand a text cloaked in an unknown history and still encounter in it a transcendent faith that animates life in the present? Many historical and theological aspects of Christian spirituality that are still operative in communities of faith are losing traction among swathes of the population, especially younger generations. Their premises have been called into question; the metaphors are dead; the symbols appear unable to mediate grace; and the ideas appear untenable. For example, is the human species really saved by the blood of Jesus on the cross? What does it mean to be resurrected from the dead? How does the Spirit unify if the church is so divided? On the other hand, the positive experiences and insights that accrued over time and added depth to Christian spirituality are being lost because they lack critical appropriation for our time. For example, has asceticism been completely lost in present-day spirituality or can we find meaning for it today? Do the mystics live in another universe, or can we find mystical dimensions in religious consciousness today? Does monasticism bear meaning for those who live outside the walls?

This series addresses these questions with a three-fold strategy. The historical first step introduces the reader to individuals who represent key ideas, themes, movements, doctrinal developments, or remarkable distinctions in theology, ethics, or spirituality. This first section will equip readers with a sense of the context of the authorship and a grammar for understanding the text.

Second, the reader will encounter the witnesses in their own words. The selected excerpts from the authors' works have exercised great influence in the history of Christianity. Letting these texts speak for themselves will enable readers to encounter the wisdom and insight of these classics anew. Equipped with the necessary background and language from the introduction, students of theology will bring the questions and concerns of their world into contact with the world of the authors. This move personalizes the objective historical context and allows the existential character of the classic witness to appear. The goal is not the study of the exact meaning of ancient texts, as important as that is. That would require a task outside the scope of this series. Recommended readings will be provided for those who wish to continue digging into this important part of interpretation. These classic texts are not presented as comprehensive representations of their authors but as statements of basic characteristic ideas that still have bearing on lived experience of faith in the twenty-first century. The emphasis lies on existential depth of meaning rather than adequate representation of an historical period which can be supplemented by other sources.

Finally, each volume also offers a preliminary interpretation of the relevance of the author and text for the present. The methodical interpretations seek to preserve the past historical meanings while also bringing them forward in a way that is relevant to life in a technologically developed and pluralistic secular culture. Each retrieval looks for those aspects that can open realistic possibilities for viable spiritual meaning in current lived experience. In the unfolding wisdom of the many volumes, many distinct aspects of the Christian history of spirituality converge into a fuller, deeper, more far-reaching, and resonant language that shows what in our time has been taken for granted, needs adjustment, or has been lost (or should be). The series begins with fifteen volumes but, like Cassian's *Conferences*, the list may grow.

About the Editors

ROGER HAIGHT, a Visiting Professor at Union Theological Seminary in New York, has written several books in the area of fundamental theology. A graduate of the University of Chicago, he is a past president of the Catholic Theological Society of America.

ALFRED PACH III is an Associate Professor of Medical Sciences and Global Health at the Hackensack Meridian School of Medicine. He has a Ph.D. from the University of Wisconsin in Madison and an MDiv in Psychology and Religion from Union Theological Seminary.

AMANDA AVILA KAMINSKI is an Assistant Professor of Theology at Texas Lutheran University, where she also serves as Director of the Program in Social Innovation and Social Entrepreneurship. She has written extensively in the area of Christian spirituality.

Past Light on Present Life:
Theology, Ethics, and Spirituality

Roger Haight, SJ, Alfred Pach III,
and *Amanda Avila Kaminski,* series editors

Available titles: